TILL DEBT DUE US PART

The Step-by-Step Guide to Getting Out of Debt and Managing Your Money

by Derek A. Marquis
Illustrations by Calvin Grondahl

D.C. Publishers & Management, L.C.

TILL DEBT DUE US PART
THE STEP-BY-STEP GUIDE
TO GETTING OUT OF DEBT AND
MANAGING YOUR MONEY

PRINTED IN THE UNITED STATES OF AMERICA
ISBN 1-883163-23-4

D.C. Publishers & Management, L.C.

Acknowledgments

Writing a book on debt elimination and personal finance, at first glance, would seem like an easy enough project. Most would agree that such a text could simply begin by examining the reasons we as Americans are in so much debt, help the reader set up some sort of a workable budget and then maybe suggest something along the lines of a savings plan. Of course at this point, reality would begin to set in. After all, how could the one subject that causes more headache, heartache, and heartburn than any other be that easy? For most of us, the only thing we understand about money is that we never have enough of it. Throw in Federal Form 4789 (CTR) and the Expedited Funds Availability Act, Public Laws 93-495, 95-109, 99-361 and the hundreds of other debt, credit and finance related "laws" that govern the world as we know it and the average person's head begins to spin.

For helping me through *my* occasional stages of dizziness, I would like to thank the following organizations, agencies and individuals: Associated Credit Bureaus, Inc., based in Washington, D.C., and Equifax based in Atlanta, Georgia for their contributions to Chapter Six, as well as the Federal Trade Commission, the Federal Deposit Insurance Corporation, the Board of Governors of the Federal Reserve System, the Committee on Banking, Finance and Urban Affairs, The Department of the Treasury and the Internal Revenue Service.

Kudos to David Hewlett who developed the "Target" personal finance computer software program available as an accompaniment to this text and to my editor James P. Bell. Thanks to Randy Moore who designed the cover, Mel Rogers of Perfect Pitch Communications, and to syndicated editorial cartoonist, Calvin Grondahl, for helping to bring a little humor to what, for most of us, is an otherwise painful topic.

A special thank you, also, to the two most important people on this project; my wife, Colleen, for her countless hours in front of the computer keyboard, and to my daughter, Kylie, both of whom, without their continued love and support this book would have never become a reality.

TILL DEBT DUE US PART

The Step-by-Step Guide to Getting Out of Debt and Managing Your Money

Contents

Introduction

The 1990s is rapidly becoming the decade where true status is not a BMW in the driveway but rather owning your own home free and clear and maintaining a zero balance on your credit cards. It's true. Pick up virtually any newspaper or magazine, or turn on any newscast, and you will find that Americans, in record numbers, are turning away from the spending craze of the 1980s to what is being called fiscal responsibility in the 1990s.

Installment debt and credit card balances are being paid off at a rate that makes the banking and retail industries cringe. Beginning in 1992 and continuing well into 1993, Americans were trading in their 13% and 15% home mortgages financed at 30 years for 15 year terms at 7½% and 8%. Economic analysts claim the recessionary climate of the late 1980s and early 1990s is turning around. They say the average American is finally getting ahead and is actually saving money, rather than spending it.

So now you are asking yourself, "If things are going so well, why does everyone seem so miserable?" A recent CBS News Poll even showed that 32% of Americans feel they are worse off now than they were in 1988. Only 23% say they are better off. The U.S. Census Bureau echoes those sentiments reporting more than 35.7 million people are currently living below the federal poverty line—more than at any time since 1964.

One of the reasons for what you and I would call the economic analysts' transparent enthusiasm can be found in the averages, as averages typically are not an accurate reflection of reality. You see, most statistics, as they are reported, are not talking about you, me, your neighbor across the street or your Uncle Eb in Orlando. They are talking about all of us lumped and averaged together.

For example, a family making $15,000 a year combined with a family making $300,000 averages to $157,500 each. Not too bad! What is too bad is that your banker won't qualify you to buy a home on what these analysts say the average income is. All that matters is what *your* income is!

The reasons also go beyond the averages. Some of the reasons can be found in the perceptions or how you read the numbers. There are, in fact, many out there who make a reasonable living by today's standards and thus should be happy and getting ahead but are not because their debt load has become overwhelming. They are often behind in their payments and barely get by from paycheck to paycheck. The statistics still show, though, that they have a great income ... more than ever before!

Once again, statistics and reality butt heads. Add to this mix, corporate layoffs in record numbers, depressed housing markets throughout much of the country, and the millions of people who simply have more going out than they do coming in each month, and the picture all of a sudden doesn't look quite so rosy.

It is for *these* individuals, the ones about whom the analysts are *not* speaking, that this book is meant. It is a book about being free: free to do what you want, when you want, and how you want, without the burden of debt or financial

uncertainty weighing you down. You have the right to be happy. You have the means to be successful, and you have the ability to take control of your own life.

You, and only you, can take the action necessary to shape your future and mold your destiny. With the right plan, a little motivation, and a lot of self-control, you, like thousands of others, can take charge of your financial future. Whether you want to break the chains of unmanageable debt, control your spending, save for your children's education, or just establish a little nest egg, the chapters that follow are written for you.

Even if you are now living from paycheck to paycheck, if you have judgements against you, or if the bank is repossessing your car, this book can provide you with a program that will lead to relief and put you on the road to financial security. Understand, though, that this is not a magical formula or an overnight success scheme. It is, instead, a proven, step-by-step program that, if followed, will systematically help you eliminate your debts and provide you with financial freedom.

The plan and steps outlined in this book follow the premise that *you* must come first. Before your creditors and before your bill collectors, *you* are your number one priority. Although this plan *will* require some sacrifice, you *will not* need to drastically reduce your standard of living or your lifestyle. Doing that would only defeat the purpose of this program and result in a reversion to your old practices of uncontrolled spending and an uncertain financial future.

Also, as you are following this personal finance course and debt elimination system, keep in mind that all you owe is some money. You are not a bad person. You just got yourself into debt, and you will get yourself out of debt. Just because you owe some money does not mean you have to put your happiness on hold. This is your life. Enjoy the journey!

There are four basic types of individuals:

1. Those who are so overwhelmed by their debts that they are just trying to get through the day without running into a bill collector or having another fight with their spouse over where all the money went. The only way out these individuals see is something drastic, unless, of course, that magazine sweepstakes award comes soon.

2. Those who are not necessarily overwhelmed by their debts, but who can never seem to get ahead financially. They meet their payments with relative ease, but still, there never seems to be anything extra. These people are living paycheck-to-paycheck saying, "If I could only get ahead."

3. Those who really aren't having any immediate problems with their debts or credit, but who feel the potential for problems is there if they don't get a better grasp on their money and what they are doing with it.

4. And finally, there are a few people out there who have all the money they could ever need or want, and never have any reason to worry about their debts or credit.

"Isn't that us?"

If you fall into the fourth category, give me a call. I can always make room for new friends. If, however, you fall into one of the first three categories, this book is for you.

No longer must you live from week to week, paycheck to paycheck, wondering how long it will be before the "repo" man comes to take your car, your furniture, or your house. No longer must you use your hard earned money to make payments on things you bought yesterday, but never have time to enjoy today. Finally, you can do with your money as you please.

And for those of you feeling fairly comfortable right now but wondering what tomorrow has in store—you can now be assured that tomorrow will be <u>even</u> <u>better</u> than today.

The Effects of Debt

Debt and guilt are the most destructive forces anyone can ever experience. No one really knows which is worse. For the purposes of this book, however, we will assume you are guilt-free and will concentrate on your debt instead. The objective of this book is not to check to see if you have the right symptoms—and then tell you, "Yes, you're in debt," or "Yes, your financial future looks uncertain"—but rather to show you, step-by-step, how to remedy the situation.

Realize also that you are not alone. Millions upon millions of people are just as stressed-out over their finances as you are. Being owned by the bill collector keeps them awake at night, just like it does you. They sleep when they should be out

working and wish they were home sleeping when they are on the job. And to top it off, everyone of them goes home each night thinking, "Tomorrow will be better."

Another effect of debt is that it makes your life an open book. Those around you not only see the stresses you are under, but they feel them as well. There are some things you just can't hide. And if the bill collector doesn't get you, the ulcers will.

If you are deeply in debt, you know all too well the feeling of living on the edge, always worrying and never relaxing or enjoying life.

Personal pride and dignity drive all of us to try to provide the finest things for ourselves and our families. But if you're a slave to debt, the feeling of your stomach tightening and maybe even a tear being shed when you have to say, "Not today, maybe tomorrow," is probably not something new. Now is the time to put all of that in the past. Erase the bill collector from your Christmas card list once and for all. He's not worth the stamp.

In a recent interview, world renowned psychologist Dr. Joyce Brothers made the comment that money problems in a marriage relationship can make for a violent battlefield. She said that all too often, either one partner takes too much blame upon him or herself, or one simply doesn't take his or her fair share.

In line with Dr. Brothers' comments, debt and financial stresses have become one of the leading factors contributing to today's alarmingly high divorce rate. In fact, the American Bar Association estimates that 89% of all divorces can be directly attributed to financial problems. No longer, it seems, is the vow "Till Death Do Us Part," ... but rather "Till Debt Due Us Part."

Who Is This Book For?

If you are in debt or in any way unsure about your financial future, this book is for you. If you have been thinking about how to pay your home mortgage off early or if you are just thinking about refinancing or purchasing your own home, this book can help. Or perhaps you just want to have enough left over at the end of the month so you can put a little extra money away in savings instead of continually living from paycheck to paycheck. Again, this book has the answers.

Regardless of your age, marital status, sex, nationality, or religious preference, the steps found in these pages will work for you. With desire, patience, self-control, and the information you have in your hands, you can soon be debt free, saving more money than you ever thought possible and achieving the financial goals most only dare to dream about. By the end of Chapter Three, in fact, you will begin to see the light at the end of the tunnel!

The key to making this plan work is the best part. There is no miracle formula or hidden secret. The key won't be found in the materials sold on late night cable television or from the corner palm reader. The key is you! You can accomplish anything you want in life. Once you have a particular goal or dream in mind—with the right tools—you can fulfill that goal and watch that dream become reality by

straightforward commitment and total conviction.

What Can This Book Do For Me?

This book is not an overnight success deal or get-rich-quick scam. Rather, it is a step-by-step, practical guide to helping you overcome the financial pressures that are weighing you down. We won't talk about selling off your first-born or drastically changing your lifestyle in order to get ahead.

What we will talk about is a proven system that, if followed as outlined, will lead you to debt free living. No matter how pessimistic you might be at first, after you begin applying the principles and strategies outlined in the following pages, you will begin to see exactly why so many people are so excited about these ideas.

No longer will you have to do a juggling act with your checkbook or wonder from week to week how you are going to make ends meet. With this book, you will learn how to set up a realistic budget, enhance the credit you currently have, and repair any credit you may have destroyed in the past.

Best of all, the steps outlined in this book will show you how to set up a repayment schedule that will allow you to cut years off the time it would normally take you to get out of debt, *without* **forcing you to spend any more money than you already are.** And if you don't have credit, it will show you how to get what you need to survive in today's world.

With the information found herein, no longer will the three "P's"—pride, prestige, and your peers—control your life. Your personal pride and prestige will come in knowing that you don't owe anyone a dime. And when that is accomplished, rest assured, your peers, neighbors, friends, and family will all want to know your secret.

What Do I Need To Use This System?

You may approach the contents of this book in any way that works for you or according to your current needs and desires. Browse through the book before you begin, just to get a feel for what lies ahead. Then read Chapters One and Two and set your goals: personal and financial. From there, you can either follow the course systematically or jump from chapter to chapter according to your interests.

As you begin, there are a few things you will need in order to make this system work smoothly. Luckily, everything needed is inexpensive and easily obtainable, and, in fact, is probably lying around your house somewhere. You don't need an office, a desk, or a filing cabinet. You will, however, need an 8½ x 11 inch folder or a three-ring binder. You can pick the folder up at any variety store for under 25¢.

Keep your folder or binder in a safe and handy place. It will be used regularly to take notes, keep records, and file correspondence with creditors.

You will also need some paper and something to write with. Raid the kid's school bag. You might also want to get a small hand-held calculator. Again, your local variety store should have one for under $5.

You do not need to rush out and buy a computer. There is a Till Debt Due Us Part personal finance computer software program known as "Target" available to accompany this text, but buying or using the software is not a pre-requisite to achieving success with this book.

Should you decide to use the "Target" software and cannot find it at your local bookstore or computer software store, there are order forms in the back of this book. If you want to use "Target" and don't have a computer, call your local library, community college, quick print, or copy center. Computers can be used on-site at these locations for a few dollars per hour—and often for free.

The "Target" program will allow you to automatically set up income and expense statements, monthly budgets, savings plans, and amortization schedules for your home mortgage or other consumer debts. Target also manages a convenient computerized checkbook register as well as debt elimination schedules for all of your bills.

The only other items you will need are a quiet place to read, work, and think—and a positive attitude.

With that ... you're ready to begin.

Chapter One

What Is Debt?

To get profit without risk, experience without danger, and reward without work, is as impossible as it is to live without being born. - A.P. Gouthey

As Webster puts it, debt is the condition of owing. It doesn't matter what you owe, how much you owe, or who you owe it to ... if you owe, you are in debt.

If a neighbor helped you build a deck last summer with the understanding that you would help him shovel snow this winter, you are in debt to your neighbor. You owe him an act of service. If a friend spends an hour helping you study for a test with the understanding that you will spend an hour showing her how to set up her new computer, you owe her your time.

As you can see, being in debt is not limited to the almighty dollar; rather, it can be extended far beyond monetary realms. For the purposes of this book, however, we will disregard debts of service or time and concentrate on the condition of owing money. The most common forms of debt are bank loans and credit cards. But there are other ways to get yourself into debt as well. Remember, it doesn't matter how much you end up owing—if you owe, it is debt. And debt added to debt only makes for more debt.

Let's get creative. How many different ways can you think of to go into debt? As you are reading over the following list, think of some of the debts you have that don't fall into the simple categories of bank loans and VISA cards.

- For your parents' 30th anniversary you send them on a trip to Hawaii, charging the plane tickets on your airline credit card.

- One of the ladies in the office is having a baby. Everyone pitches in a dollar to buy her a gift, but you don't have any cash with you, so you tell the person buying the gift that you'll pay your dollar tomorrow.

- You walk across the street for a burger and milk shake with a friend from the office and, oops, you forgot your wallet. He buys ... you owe.

- You charge a new dress, hat, and shoes on your Saks Fifth Avenue card.

- You're in a transition between jobs and don't have any insurance. Your daughter gets sick, you take her to the doctor, and he sets up a repayment schedule over the next three months.

- You charge a new color monitor for your computer on your Sears card.

- You fill up your car's gas tank and put it on your Texaco card.

- Tuition is due, your government grant hasn't come yet, so you borrow the money from mom and dad.

- You're short on cash and the bank is closed for the holiday, so you tap a friend for ten bucks.

- That old car just won't make it through the winter. The local Chevy dealer has a deal you just can't pass up and he'll do the financing with "No payments until Spring." Like magic, you have a new car!

- You know your tax returns are coming, and this is the last week of that sale at the lawn sprinkler shop. No problem—the terms of the sale are: "No payments until May."

The list goes on and on. Again, there are countless ways of getting into debt. For most of us, we don't worry much about owing the office pool or the person who bought us that soft drink at work. We've got "real" debt to be concerned with. But for others, every dollar does matter.

Regardless of how large or small *your* debt load may be, if you are in over your head, the effects of the debt will most likely be the same.

Too many people are in situations that are already causing serious harm, or that at least have the potential to cause harm, to themselves, to their relationships with others, and to their credit standing. Far too many are being forced by their debts to live from paycheck to paycheck, with their checking account balances always at zero. The only miracle in the lives of these people is the one called the "overdraft protection" attached to their checking accounts. And that actually just adds to their debt.

Real Life

It is important to point out that the vast majority of people who have unmanageable debt cannot be written off as irresponsible, lazy, careless, or immature money managers. In fact, financial counselors estimate that most who are in this situation got there through little or no fault of their own. Unexpected medical expenses, unemployment, a child's college expenses, a death in the family, divorce, and separation are just a few of the reasons cited.

Understand that there are, and will continue to be, times when debt becomes temporarily necessary. And you cannot feel guilty for taking care of these unexpected expenses. If there is a death in the family and you have to charge the plane tickets to get home for the funeral, then charge the plane tickets. If tuition for your children's college has taken its toll on the bank account and you need a new clothes dryer, there is nothing wrong with charging the dryer on your Sears card and paying for it over the next 13 months. These are the realities of life.

Hopefully, however, once you apply the principles found in this book and you are out of debt, you will be able to pay cash for that dryer. But in the meantime, just be realistic about your spending practices.

It is also reasonable to accept that once you are totally debt free, there will be nothing wrong with paying for dinner with your American Express card or filling up your gas tank with your Exxon card. What you need to avoid in the future is not the use of credit, but rather problem and compulsive spending that results in excessive debt.

A while back we had some friends come to visit from out of town. Over dinner we began talking about some of the things discussed in this book, and our conversation turned to mortgages, as this couple had recently purchased a home in Las Vegas. The point was made that under the terms set up by the mortgage company, they would be paying three times the value of their home in interest over the course of the loan. And that is *in addition* to the principal they'd be paying.

Another interesting comment that came up was that after taking into account their house, car, and boat payments (and the other little odds and ends they were paying for each month), if for some reason they

were to be without an income for any period of time, they could only survive for about one month. Of course we all conceded that if this situation were to arise, we would change our lifestyles in order to make ends meet. But still, it is frightening to think about the thousands of people who are unexpectedly faced with an abrupt loss of income each and every day, with nowhere to turn.

This is the purpose of this book: to show you how you can, once and for all, get the debt monkey off of your back, and to provide you with the ammunition needed to conquer life's unexpectancies.

Why Do We Go Into Debt?

In 1980, the federal debt of the United States was at $900 billion. Now, just over a decade later that same federal debt is at 4.2 TRILLION dollars. If you were to break that down, your family's share would be over $61,000. And it's not stopping there.

The nation's debt continues to increase at a rate of $13,000 each second. That's $780,000 a minute; $46 MILLION per hour, and an increase of $1 BILLION every day! *USA Today* reported in late 1992, in a series on "Capitol Cash," that the House of Representatives alone costs taxpayers $80,000 an hour — 24 hours a day, 365 days a year. To find out where all that money is going to, you'd have to do a detailed analysis of 7,473 pages of House finance records.

Keep in mind that all of this spending continues even as every politician in Washington vows to do everything in his or her power to decrease the national debt and balance the budget.

The federal debt, in fact, is now so large that interest on the debt is the second-largest item on the government spending list; $292 billion in fiscal 1992. And if there is one thing that most economists seem to agree on, it is that the change from the Bush administration to the Clinton administration is having little impact on reducing the federal deficit. Spending more than we take in seems to be as American as apple pie.

Before you get up in arms over the federal budget deficit, keep in mind that we as consumers are doing exactly the same thing as the federal government. Many of us know that we are already in over our heads. We talk about bringing our own financial houses in order, but still, we continue to charge millions and Millions and MILLIONS of dollars <u>every day</u> of <u>every week</u>.

So if we know and fully understand the devastating effects of debt, why then are so many still getting deeper and deeper into debt? There is a plague on the wall in the office building where I work that reads, "The chief cause of failure and unhappiness is trading what we want most for what we want at the moment."

Perhaps one of the reasons we continue to add to our debt can be found in our attempt to "keep up with the Jones." The only problem is that the Jones no longer seem to be good enough. Now it's the Rockefellers and the Vanderbilts we are chasing.

"The Rockefellers," you say. "That's ridiculous. I don't need an office plaza in downtown Manhattan. All I need is a wide screen television set for the football season." Regardless of what it is you want, or what it is you think you need, if you are living from paycheck to paycheck, the results of falling into the "more, more, more" syndrome will be the same.

Let's make it clear right here that there is nothing wrong with improving your station in life. In fact, that is what this book is all about. I am all in favor of

"Oh no, the Jones are digging a deeper hole for themselves than we are!"

success, nice homes, cars, wide screen television sets, etc. I am not, however, in favor of the stresses and strains that accompany the debt connected with these things.

It doesn't matter if it's a $500,000 house and a $35,000 car that are getting you down, or just a $100 loan from a friend. Debt is debt. It has the same effects on everyone. Nobody likes it, nobody wants it, everybody is stressed out by it, and everybody wishes somebody would show them the miracle formula to help them get rid of it.

No matter how bad your debts might be making you feel, you need to understand that there *is* hope and there *is* a way out. Nobody owns you. It may seem that they do when you have more money going out each month than you have coming in, but the fact is that it is against the law for any person or any organization to own another person. So, once and for all, get the idea that you are owned by your creditors out of your system. You are not.

Not only are *things* not as bad as you might think, but *you* are not as bad as you might think. You need to understand and fully accept that you are not only a *good* person, but a *great* person. So you owe some money. Big deal. Life goes on. It may weigh you down at times, it may stress you out at times, but owing money does not mean you are a second-class citizen.

All you owe is some money. You don't owe your self-esteem, your pride, or your right to be alive. Money is just an instrument of trade, an instrument to barter with. Don't let a 6 x 2½ inch piece of green paper ruin your day.

Getting Out
The Way You Got In

You didn't wake up this morning suddenly overwhelmed by your debts or your uncertain financial future. Maybe you didn't realize that you were overwhelmed until this morning, but the fact is, it didn't happen overnight.

You might have started out bumming a few bucks from your friends when you were a teenager. Or you might have started when you first set out on your own, determined to make it without mom and dad's help. But regardless of how it happened, it happened ... one day at a time. And just as the debts grew in size, one day at a time, they can disappear.

With that understanding, you must make a commitment to yourself; a commitment that, for the rest of today, you will not incur a single additional dollar of debt. This shouldn't be a big deal, because the commitment is only for one day. What happens tomorrow, next Tuesday, or next December is not important. All that is important is that you do not incur a single dollar or even a penny of debt today.

Anyone can make it through one day. Just plan for it. Take your credit cards out of your wallet. Take the bus instead of the taxi. Have yogurt for lunch instead of a burger, fries, and Cherry Coke. It doesn't matter how you do it. Just do it.

Don't use that gas card when you fill up today. Use cash or your checkbook. If you don't have cash and can't find your checkbook, go to the bank and get cash. (Only get as much as you will realistically need. If you get more, you'll probably spend more.) Don't bum a dollar from anyone at work. And don't go looking at new cars on your lunch break. Sure, life will be a little inconvenient at times, but remember, it's only one day. Prove to yourself that you can make it through one day without getting further into debt!

Don't make any excuses. It won't take long—in fact, only until tomorrow—before you will be <u>not</u> going into debt, one day at a time. Then, when you wake up tomorrow, recommit yourself ... not for a week, not for a month, but for the rest of the day. You will be amazed at how easy life is when you take it one day at a time.

Let me reiterate what was said at the beginning of this book. To those who are patient and apply the principles found in each chapter, the good life *will* come. You won't have to keep up with anybody else.

You will be so busy enjoying the new wealth you've uncovered by being free from debt and by knowing what your financial future holds that you will not have any time to worry about what the Jones or the Rockefellers have parked in their driveways.

Chapter Two

Where Am I Today?

If you don't know where you are going,
you'll probably end up somewhere else.
- Lawrence Peter

The entire purpose of this book is to prepare you to win every battle you might face as you embark on your journey toward financial freedom. But before you can really begin your journey, you will need to get an appraisal or evaluation of where you are today.

Being honest with yourself will be a key factor to your success. If you are married, have a family, or share income and expenses with another person, it might be a good idea to sit down with them and go through this chapter together.

To begin with, write down three things you want—things you really want. Don't spend too much time thinking about them—just write them down. Of course, make getting out of debt the first thing on the list, followed by two others.

Getting out of debt may not be the <u>most</u> important thing on your list, but if you accomplish that, it stands to reason that many of the other things will come so much easier. So grab a pen and let's get started.

What Do I Really Want?

1. <u>To be 100% debt free!</u> _____

   _____

2. _____

   _____

3. _____

   _____

Now, without dwelling on past failures, shortcomings, mistakes, or the like, quickly write down what accomplishments you are most proud of. These things do not have to be feats of great strength or things that your peers have "recognized" you for. Just write down whatever it is you are proud of. (For some people, just getting to work on time is a big accomplishment.)

Accomplishments I'm Most Proud Of!

1. _____

   _____

2. _____

   _____

3. _____

   _____

Before you go any further I must address those of you who are just thinking about the answers to these questions but not writing them down. Thoughts will not

suffice! You must perform actions to reap the rewards that are awaiting you. Yes, you may be able to get through the first few steps of getting out of debt or managing your finances *just* by relying on memory, but you don't want to *just* get by. You want to arrive!

It will be much easier to accomplish the steps that follow if you begin writing down your plan of action now. Prove to yourself that you are committed to doing whatever it takes to accomplish your goals—commit yourself on paper. If you are going to succeed at this, you are going to have to change your mindset and do things a little differently than you are accustomed to.

For those of you who have committed yourself in writing, congratulations! You're heading in the right direction. For those of you who haven't, stop right here, find a pencil, and go back to the beginning of this chapter and start out fresh, with new conviction. If you don't want to write in your book, now would be a good time to get out your folder, paper, and pen. Remember, this is a <u>step-by-step</u> guide, not only for getting out of debt, but for accomplishing anything you want in life. You must follow these steps to reach your full potential.

Now, on to the next step. Make a spontaneous list of how you would like your future to unfold. Again, just write down whatever comes to mind. Be brief. Don't spend too much time thinking about it. Include in this list everything you would like to accomplish in the next ten years: a new house, a high-paying position, a trip around the world. Make this list as long as you please. Just write

"Ok, let's set some goals to get out of debt."

things down as they come to mind. Add to the list as often as you like. Tomorrow you will think of things you didn't think of today. You can go back anytime and add to the list.

After your list is complete, or at least close to being complete, go back and prioritize the items you've listed. Place a number next to each item in order of its importance or in order of what you would like to accomplish first, second, third, and so on.

Try not to make all of your goals material in nature. Balance the material desires with other things you want, such as love, an exercise routine, more time with the family, etc.

How I Would Like My Future To Unfold

1. Be out of debt.

—

—

—

—

—

—

—

Don't Stop Now

Now that you have on paper some of your goals and desires, you can pull from that list or come up with other ideas as you make your six-month goals, one-year goals, five-year goals, and so on. If you'd like, you can make copies of these goals and keep them in your folder or tape them to you refrigerator or mirror.

Don't worry about how you are going to accomplish all of these things. Just think positive! Think success! What a great feeling to be on the way to debt free living! Make your goals fun, make them exciting, but keep them realistic. Don't let anything stand in your way. You really can have everything you want out of life! It is all up to you.

Six-Month Goals

1. Master each step necessary to get out of debt.

2. _____

3. _____

4. _____

5. _____

One-Year Goals

1. Be closer to being debt free.

2. _____

3. _____

4. _____

5. _____

Five-Year Goals

1. Have all my debts paid off.

2. _____

3. _____

4. _____

5. _____

Congratulations! You have successfully completed the first step toward eliminating your debts and taking charge of your financial future. "But I still owe money," you cry. Be patient. Putting your thoughts on paper is just the *first* step. Don't worry if you can't see how each individual step is going to help you reach your goal. You will be amazed at how they will all come together. A single piece of a puzzle never makes much sense by itself. But when all the pieces are put together in an orderly fashion, the picture springs to life and can be enjoyed for years to come.

Now, we are going to pick one goal from your six-month list and concentrate on it. We'll call it your "Target Goal." And guess which one we'll start with? That's right, getting out of debt. And after you accomplish that goal, you will move on, with the next goal on your list becoming your target goal, and so on. It is crucial that you focus on only one goal at a time. If you try to accomplish everything at once, you will be consumed and overwhelmed, and the task will likely become overpowering. That doesn't mean you should forget the other goals. In fact, you should review your goals daily as a reminder of the great things you have to look forward to.

You may even be able to start working on some of your short-term goals while focusing on your target goal of getting out of debt. For example, if some of your goals are to be more positive, more relaxed, or exercise regularly, working on these goals can actually help you achieve your larger goal of getting out of debt.

Remember, you can be the master of your own mind. But before you can be its master your mind must be trained. At the beginning of each day, in your folder or three-ring binder, write down what you plan to accomplish that day. At the end of the day, go back and write down what you did accomplish.

You may find it easier to make the next day's plans each night before you go to bed. *When* you make your plans is not important. What *is* important is that you review your plans each morning before you begin your day. It is crucial that you do this the first thing in the morning while you are fresh and before anything can distract you. In addition to this daily ritual, plan and evaluate at the end of each week and month as well. Remember to keep your thoughts positive and concentrate on your accomplishments. Don't write down the things you failed to do. Everything in your file should be totally positive.

Three Steps To Success

In the chapters that follow, there will be many charts and schedules that you will need to fill in. Don't get discouraged—you can't just read your debts away. You have to put into *action* the steps that will lead you toward accomplishing your goals.

But as was mentioned at the beginning of the chapter, before you can actually do anything about your current situation, you have to know where you are. You also have to know where you want to be tomorrow. And, finally, you have to have a plan to get you there.

These three steps are each equally important. After all, if you don't know where you are, you'll never know when or if you get there! And if you don't have a plan, chances are you're just spinning your wheels and getting deeper and deeper into a rut. Again, the steps to success are as follows:

1. Figure out where you are today.

2. Decide where you want to be tomorrow.

3. Develop or find a plan of action to take you there.

These three steps are the same no matter what it is you want to accomplish. Today you will use them to get out of debt. Tomorrow you will use them to unlock the hidden secrets and dreams that keep you going from day to day.

Chapter Three

Debt Elimination

I've been rich and I've been poor.
Rich is better. - Sophie Tucker

The following chapters will deal with everything from cleaning up your credit to establishing a realistic budget and savings plan. But before you get to all of that, you need to get an accurate picture of where you are today and then implement the actual steps that are going to help you eliminate your debts. The debt elimination system outlined in this chapter is extremely easy to understand and just as easy to follow. It will, however, require an enormous amount of self-control, a lot of patience, and, of course, some sacrifice.

There are no hidden secrets here, just logical, step-by-step guidelines that, if followed, will lead you to debt free living.

You may, in fact, already be following many of the steps discussed in this chapter. But now it's time to go a step further. With the information found here, you will be able to maximize everything you do, and subsequently see results much faster than you ever thought possible.

By the end of this chapter you will finally be able to see the light at the end of the tunnel. You will know exactly, to the day, when you will be debt free. But remember, your journey is not over when your debts are paid off. You will still have to be consistent in your efforts to cleanup your credit reports, establish a new and enhanced credit profile and begin a savings plan that will help you meet your future goals. And most of all, you'll need to guard against falling back into debt in the future.

The Rules

Life is full of rules and regulations. Your debt elimination plan is no exception. In order for you to realize the sweet successes awaiting you, you will have to follow four important rules. Do not discount any of them. Full compliance is crucial to your success. They are as follows:

1. Stop unnecessary spending! Never again buy anything if it has interest attached. If you need it, pay cash. If you can't pay cash, it must wait.

2. For now, cease contributions to savings accounts, IRAs, thrift plans, etc.

3. Be positive! In everything you do and everything that happens to you, look at the bright side of things. Go out of your way to be happy and positive.

4. Don't be a fanatic! Realize that you will have to be flexible and that there *will* be obstacles as you begin to put these steps into practice. Use common sense when emergencies arise.

Let's probe each of these rules more closely.

Stop unnecessary spending! I hope you're not asking why. But in case you are, the explanation is simple. Your spending got you where you are today. It simply makes sense that eliminating your debts will be much harder if you continue to rack up more bills.

You also must avoid interest like the plague! Interest is the fee you are charged for the privilege of buying an item with credit or borrowing money. You pay it every time you borrow money—whether it's to buy a car, a boat or furniture, or whether you're just using your credit cards. Interest is what keeps the lender or seller in business. Interest pays their overhead and their payroll, and puts a handsome profit in their pockets.

No longer are you going to help these lenders get rich by making yourself poor. (If you have a problem with excessive, impulsive spending, you will want to pay particular attention to the information in Chapter Eight.)

Cease contributions to savings accounts, IRAs, company thrift plans, etc. It doesn't make sense to be receiving a 5%, 6% or even 10% return on your money when you are paying 22% on your debts. If you currently have money in such plans, that's great! That money will play a big part in your debt elimination plan. But until your debts are all paid off, put your savings on hold. Then after you are debt free, you will be able to use the same steps found in this chapter, and chapters to come, to return to your savings plan—and put away more money than you ever thought possible.

Keep a positive attitude! The road to success is so much easier and enjoyable if you will keep your mindset positive. Go out of your way to be happy. Those around you won't be able to figure out what is different about you. When little things are getting them down, you will be rolling with the punches and having a good time doing it.

Why is this such an important step? Because, as you will see, the old cliché, "Whatever the mind can conceive and believe, it can achieve," really is true. Those who are successful in life have found a way to maintain a positive attitude. There is a special magnetism about people who know what they want, go after it and get back up when they fall. It's time for you to become one of these magnetic people.

Change your mindset, and don't let little things get you uptight or stressed out. Remember, <u>success</u> <u>follows</u> <u>those</u> <u>who</u> <u>keep</u> <u>a</u> <u>positive</u> <u>attitude</u>!

Don't be a fanatic! When it comes to implementing the steps found in this book, realize that there will have to be some flexibility. There will always be setbacks. Plans will have to be changed and obstacles will have to be overcome. When you get sidetracked, evaluate the situation, take a deep breath, and get back on target as quickly as possible. The key is to use common sense, good judgement and self-control.

With these four steps as a guide, it is time for you to get out of debt once and for all. First on the list, you will need a system of keeping your bills and financial records organized. Although crucial to your success, this need not be a time consuming task. In fact, the Internal Revenue Service estimates that if you were to file <u>all</u> of the major schedules associated with the 1040 Tax Form, you would spend only 26 hours and 20 minutes a year keeping the records needed for those schedules. That breaks out to just seconds a day.

I find an alphabetized, accordion-type file works well for me. Again, these can be picked up at the neighborhood variety store for under $5. If that is not feasible, make a couple of folders out of construction paper or cardboard.

Just be sure you have something that you can tape, fold, or paper clip shut to keep your bills from falling out and getting misplaced. And make sure they are organized. Stuffing everything into an old shoebox is probably not the best system.

In your file, keep all of your bills, credit bureau reports, correspondence to your creditors, etc. If you have past bill stubs lying around in junk drawers or under beds, gather them together and file them. Alphabetize them for easy access. (For example, put the gas bill under "G", the car payment under "C".) Don't fret if you have two or three bills under one letter. The main idea is to keep things organized so that you can find them.

(Although perfect for bill and record keeping, your filing system will probably not suffice for storage of other important documents like wills, diaries, and birth certificates. These should be kept in a safety deposit box or fireproof strong box for safety.)

Getting Down to the Basics

NOTE: Although the information to come in this chapter may seem technical, it is really quite simple to follow. Read and reread these instructions as many times as it takes. This is the only chapter that deals with numbers so intensely. It is also the most important

chapter in the debt-elimination process. For this reason it is crucial that you not brush over this chapter lightly.

How Much Are You Worth?

Before you can begin the task of eliminating your debts and mapping out your financial future, you will need to get an accurate appraisal of where you are today—your current net worth. Unfortunately, most people have no idea what they are worth. In fact, many people can tell you what color socks they wore to their high school prom but they can't tell you what their current balance in their checking account is.

Don't be discouraged, after filling out the net worth worksheet, if you are not where you had hoped to be at this stage of your life or if current economic conditions have taken their toll on you and your pocketbook. Many people, in fact, will find that their net worth is a negative number, that they owe more on their debt than they have in cash, equity and other assets. Welcome to real life! It's not so important what numbers you come up with on this worksheet as it is just knowing where you are, currently, in your financial life.

If after filling in the following worksheet you find that you are worse off than you originally thought, don't despair. At least you will have a better idea of what you will need to do as you plan for the future. If, however, you find you are better off than you originally thought, (and many people will) don't get so excited that you put this book away and go out on a

Net Worth Worksheet
Assets

ASSETS	MARKET VALUE	ASSETS	MARKET VALUE
Cash and Cash Equivalents		**Collectibles**	
Checking account(s)	$ _____	Antiques	$ _____
Savings account(s)	_____	Art	_____
Certificate(s) of deposit . .	_____	Gold and silver	_____
Money-market account(s) .	_____	Other (stamps, etc.)	_____
Cash mngmnt. account(s)	_____		
Credit union account(s) . .	_____	**Retirement Assets**	
		IRA	_____
Stocks and Bonds		Company pension plan .	_____
Stocks	_____	401(K)	_____
Bonds	_____	Keogh	_____
Futures	_____	Savings plan	_____
Commodities	_____	Profit sharing	_____
Fixed-income securities . .	_____		
Unit trusts	_____	**Insurance**	
Mutual Funds	_____	Cash value-life insurance	_____
Options	_____	Surrender value-annuities	_____
Real-Estate Investment		**Personal Property**	
Value of home	_____	Automobiles	_____
Value of vacation home . .	_____	Boats	_____
Real-estate partnerships . .	_____	Campers/RVs	_____
Rental property	_____	Household furnishing . .	_____
Other	_____	Jewelry	_____
		Other	_____
		Total	$ _____

Liabilities

LIABILITIES	PAYOFF BALANCE	LIABILITIES	PAYOFF BALANCE
Home mortgage	$ _____	Credit lines	$ _____
Vacation home mortgage .	_____	Home equity line	_____
Other real-estate debts . . .	_____	Overdraft line	_____
Automobile loan(s)	_____	Unsecured credit line .	_____
Other installment loan(s) .	_____	Income taxes	_____
Tuition loan(s)	_____	Property taxes	_____
Credit cards:		Margin loans from brokers	_____
Bank	_____	Miscellaneous debt	_____
Retail stores	_____		
Oil companies	_____		
Other	_____	**Total**	$ _____

Net Worth

Assets . . . . $ _____

Less liabilities . . . . - _____

Net Worth . . . . =$ _____

spending spree. Remember the reasons you picked up this book in the first place.

Also, when filling out the worksheet, don't be discouraged if you don't have all or even many of the assets listed. Most people won't. It will also help to round all numbers to the nearest dollar amount. Also be sure to list current values, not values you are projecting at a later date. Finally, do not reduce the value of your assets by any debt outstanding on them. Debt will be figured in the liability section of the worksheet. (Additional net worth worksheets are in Appendix B.)

After you have an idea of where you are financially or at least what you are worth, you need to take a closer look at those items listed as liabilities or debts. Use the Debt Elimination Schedule (DES), a form provided on page 25, to outline your current "debt" situation. (There are also extra Debt Elimination Schedules in Appendix B.) List all of your debts and obligations, who they are owed to and so forth. As you are doing this you may come up with additional debts that you failed to list on your net worth worksheet. That's okay. Just be sure to list every debt on your DES that is currently outstanding.

The "Original Balance" is the original amount borrowed or financed. For credit cards, the "Original Balance" is the credit limit of the card, regardless of whether you have ever reached the limit.

The "DES Start Date" is the first day of the month in which you begin putting your debt elimination plan to work ... not the date you incurred the debt and not the date each bill is due. (Thus, if you've already paid this month's bills, the plan start date will need to be the first day of next month.) In short, the Start Date should be the same for every debt you list on your DES. The "Current Balance" is the amount it would take to pay off the debt today. And the "Monthly Payment" is the minimum or regular amount due each month. **Debts should always be listed progressively, from smallest current balance to largest.**

Be aware that the minimum monthly payment billed by some of your creditors will decrease as the balance due decreases, as is the case with credit cards and department store charge cards. Regardless of how tempting it may be to do otherwise, you need to keep paying the same amount each and every month. The reason these creditors lower your payment, or even allow you to skip a payment, is to keep you paying them your hard earned money over a longer period of time. Remember, it is *your* interest that helps to keep these guys in business. Don't let them use you.

Continue making the same monthly payment each month that you listed on your Debt Elimination Schedule when you started this plan until the debt is paid off, regardless of what you are billed down the road. (Of course, if your bill goes up, you will have to pay more. Just be sure you never pay less.)

For now, don't worry about the "Payoff Balance," the "Accrued Payment" or the "Projected Payoff" columns. These will be explained in detail later in this chapter.

Understand also that this is not a budget. That will come later. So for now don't think about income or assets, just concentrate on what is owed. Also, for

Debt Elimination Schedule
(DES)

	Creditor/Lender	Original Balance	DES Start Date	Current Balance	Monthly Payment	Payoff Balance	Accrued Payment	Projected Payoff
1								
2								
3								
4								
5								
6								
7								
8								
9								
10								
11								
12								
13								
14								
15								
16								
17								
18								
19								
20								
21								
22								
23								
24								
25								
26								
27								
28								
Totals			**N/A**			**N/A**	**N/A**	**N/A**

now, don't list anything that would be considered a monthly household expense—things like rent, lights, gas, food, etc. Keep your list to debts that can be eliminated.

The debt with the smallest current balance on your list will be referred to from here on as your "Target Debt," which simply means the debt you are zeroing in on. Again, the debt with the smallest current balance should be the first one on the list, and the debt with the largest current balance should be last on the list. The reason for listing your bills this way is simple—the smallest debt will be the easiest and the quickest to pay off. When a debt is paid off, the next one in line becomes the Target Debt.

You may first want to list your debts in your folder and then transfer them to the Debt Elimination Schedule on page 25. Whatever the case, use a pencil, as you will inevitably have to make changes. When you have all your debts listed, use a calculator to determine the totals for each column.

Are you surprised by the totals at the bottom of the "Monthly Payment" column? Can you think of anything else you would rather be using that money for?

One of the comments I often hear is that bills seem to add up overnight, and then take a lifetime to pay off. Another is that you never seem to get that many dollars' enjoyment out of the things you are still paying for. Don't be depressed by your debt load. Be assured that by the end of this book, if not by the end of this chapter, your goal of debt-free living will be well within your reach.

Now go back over your Debt Elimination Schedule to see if there is anything else that needs to be added. Are there any past due monthly bills that are being paid in time payments because the original balance was too large to pay all at once? An example of this would be a phone bill or utility bill that is being paid off little by little each month because it was too large to pay off in one lump sum.

If there is anything else you come up with, be sure to add it to your chart. Included on the next page are some debts that you may have forgotten.

By the way, don't worry if you can't come up with enough debts to fill in all the spaces on your DES. In fact, consider yourself lucky if you can't. But, even if you do fill the page and have to go on to another page, don't give up hope! It may take a little longer and require a little more sacrifice before you are totally debt free, but it will happen.

Now go back to your schedule and determine if there are any debts that you can eliminate simply by stopping the payments on them. "All of them," you say? Wrong! That is not what I'm talking about. What I am referring to is payments that can be stopped without your going to jail or, at least, without getting in trouble with the creditor.

Examples of such debt would be membership dues at the country club or a subscription to a magazine or newspaper. The only thing that will happen to you if you do stop payments on such things is that your membership will be revoked and the subscription discontinued.

Of course, be sure to let the club, magazine, or whatever know that you are canceling. Don't just stop payments without an explanation. This could result in a negative rating on your credit report. And the time may come when you will want to resume doing business with them.

If you're not sure what debts can be immediately eliminated, refer to Chapter Five. Then if you find such items on your DES get rid of them. Remember, the good life, with all of its luxuries and splendor, will come—as soon as your debts are behind you.

Possible Debts

American Express	*Friend Loans*	*Real Estate Debts*
Appliances	*Furniture*	*Record/Tape Clubs*
Bank Debit Card	*Gasoline Charges*	*Retirement*
Bank Loans	*Golf/Country Club*	*R.V. Payments*
Boat Loans	*Home Imprv. Loan*	*Sears*
Book Clubs	*Hospital Bills*	*Stereo Payments*
Car Loans	*JCPenney*	*Storage Units*
Carpet Payments	*Magazine Subscrp.*	*Student Loans*
Club Dues	*Maid/Cleaning Fees*	*Taxes Still Owed*
Computer	*MasterCards*	*Tire Store Credit*
Department Store	*Montgomery Ward*	*Travel Clubs*
Diner's Club	*Personal Loans*	*Vacation Debt*
Dentist Bills	*Phone Calling Cards*	*Video Camera*
Discover Card	*Photo Studio Bills*	*Video Clubs*
Doctor Bills	*Post Office Box*	*VISA Cards*
Family Loans	*Property Dues*	*Washer/Dryer*

Debt vs. Non-Debt

The reason we have not listed items such as rent, electricity, gas, car insurance, etc., on your DES is quite simple. These are not debts. These are living expenses. Of course, you may be able to cut back or find lower rates than what you are currently paying, but for the most part you will be making most of these payments for the rest of your life, regardless of where you are financially.

Here's an example: Car insurance is considered a normal payment or living expense instead of a debt because, like your phone bill and electricity payment,

that bill will always be there. Regardless of who you are, if you drive, you must be insured. The car <u>payment</u>, on the other hand, is a debt you *can* pay off and have behind you for good.

This approach should help you determine the difference between debt and the inescapable costs of being alive. The only exception to this rule would be your home mortgage. Although you will learn through this chapter, and the next chapter, how to pay off your mortgage in a relatively short period of time, it should be recognized that your mortgage may not be a bad debt. Your home mortgage, instead, could fall into the category of an

investment if it is building equity and increasing in value as time passes. Even so, list your mortgage on your Debt Elimination Schedule anyway. You still want to pay it off!

Income/Expenses

Before you can eliminate your debt load, there are two other things you need to be aware of. First, the income or monetary resources you have coming in each month; and, second, the expenses causing your money to go out each month.

When we talk about expenses, we are talking about anything you are paying for each month that is not included on your DES, the bills that will inevitably come regardless of where you are financially.

Again, use the forms provided to analyze where you are, and then copy them over to your personal file. Make numbers reflect after-tax totals, which are easily found on your paycheck stubs. For sources of income where taxes are paid at the end of the year, estimate the taxes that will be owed and subtract that amount from the bottom of the chart.

Now before you go any further, determine which of these monthly expenses can be cut back, or, better yet, totally eliminated. The most likely ones to eliminate are things like pay television channels, certain types of life insurance, dining out, maid/cleaning services, and anything else you are paying for each month that isn't really required to survive (refer to Chapter Five). The key is to make sure all of your living expenses are absolutely necessary to sustain life.

Once you are positive everything on your expense list is necessary, you need to see if the figures from all of your charts mesh. By mesh I mean, does the money coming in adequately cover the bills going out? To determine if they do, use your calculator to fill in the *"Monthly Earned*

Income Chart" and the *"Average Monthly Expenses Chart."* Then use the table on page 31 to see what your totals work out to be. (These charts and calculations can also be done using the Target personal finance computer software package.)

Monthly Earned Income*

Husband . . . . _____

Wife . . . . _____

Children (if helping with expenses) . . . . _____

Self-employed income aside from job . . . . _____

Bonus . . . . _____

Allowance . . . . _____

Interest on savings . . . . _____

Interest from stocks/bonds . . . . _____

Dividends . . . . _____

Rental income . . . . _____

Trust income . . . . _____

Social Security benefits . . . . _____

Veteran's benefits . . . . _____

Pension/retirement income . . . . _____

Unemployment compensation . . . . _____

Disability payments . . . . _____

Assistance payments . . . . _____

Alimony/child support . . . . _____

Gifts/non-obligatory support from family . . . . _____

Other _____ . . . . _____

Other _____ . . . . _____

Other _____ . . . . _____

Other _____ . . . . _____

Other _____ . . . . _____

Total monthly income . . . . $\underline{\hspace{2cm}}

Taxes not withheld that will need to be paid at end of the year . . . . . . _____
(This is the only money to be put in savings)

Total monthly income after taxes . . . . $\underline{\hspace{2cm}}
*List only after-tax, or net income.

Average Monthly Expenses

Rent/mortgage . . . . $ _____

Fuel/gas . . . . _____

Electricity . . . . _____

Water . . . . _____

Garbage . . . . _____

Automobile gasoline/oil/maintenance . . . . _____

Children's expenses—school lunches, fees, etc. _____

Children's expenses—lessons (piano, dance, etc.) . . . . _____

Children's expenses—other . . . . _____

Higher education/tuition/books . . . . _____

Higher education/room and board . . . . _____

Cable television/pay television channels . . . . _____

Telephone . . . . _____

Pharmacy prescriptions . . . . _____

Medical expenses . . . . _____

Taxes (not already deducted from pay) . . . . _____

Contributions/church . . . . _____

Contributions/savings . . . . _____

Contributions/other . . . . _____

Homeowners/renters insurance . . . . _____

Other property insurance . . . . _____

Disability insurance . . . . _____

Medical/health insurance . . . . _____

Life insurance . . . . _____

Auto insurance . . . . _____

Emergency fund . . . . _____

Allowances . . . . _____

Groceries . . . . _____

Dining out . . . . _____

Laundry/cleaning . . . . _____

Home/office supplies . . . . _____

Animal care . . . . _____

Recreation/entertainment . . . . _____

Travel/vacation . . . . _____

Dues . . . . _____

Subscriptions . . . . _____

Other_____ . . . . _____

Other_____ . . . . _____

Other_____ . . . . _____

Other_____ . . . . _____

Total monthly expenses . . . . $ _____

Total monthly net income (page 29) . . . . _____

Total average monthly expenses (page 30) . . . . (subtract) -_____

Difference . . . . = _____

Total of "Monthly Payments" From DES (page 25) . (subtract) -_____

Balance . . . . = _____

Targeting In

Let's hope the amount on the balance line is a positive number. If not, you will need to do one of two things ... possibly both. You will need to find a way to increase your monthly income and/or you will need to find ways to cut your monthly expenses by that amount. After all, the amount shown here is the difference between what you have coming in and what you have going out.

If you find yourself in the negative trap, you will also want to pay special attention to Chapter Five.

Accrued Payments on Your DES

If you have extra income (from the balance line of the above chart) left over each month after paying your debts and living expenses, you have two choices. Ideally that money will be added to the regular monthly payment of the first debt (your Target Debt) listed on your DES to help you get out of debt quicker.

Some people, however, may choose to use that extra money to "play and relax", save, or somehow reward themselves. The choice is yours. Sometimes we do need to pamper ourselves. Just remember, the sooner you get out of debt, the sooner you

will really be able to play and relax, save, and reward yourself.

Again, if you do decide to use any extra money to get out of debt sooner, add that extra money to the monthly payment of the first debt on your list (your Target Debt). Many people believe they should apply any excess money toward the debt with the highest interest rate. Not so! List your debts in order of the smallest current balance to the largest, regardless of interest rates. Then work toward paying the debts off in that order.

A Quick Word on Savings

If you have money in some kind of a savings account or a savings plan that can be withdrawn without giving up your firstborn, use it to pay off as many of your smaller debts as possible. For now, keep only about three months' living expenses in your savings account. Do this before you go any further. You may find that some of your smaller debts can be totally eliminated by doing this. Eliminated debts will not need to be listed on your DES.

"Use my savings? What about emergencies?" While I am a firm believer in having someplace to turn in case of unexpected emergencies, I have a hard time accepting a measly 5% or even 10%

or 12% interest on my savings when I am paying 22% on my debts. Remember, you will keep enough in savings to get you by for three months should you have an abrupt loss of income. And for other emergencies—the answer is to have a "for emergencies only" credit card.

Have a card set aside that you don't owe anything on. If an emergency arises, use the card. The benefit of, and logic behind this, should be easy to understand. If there are no emergencies, you are not out any money, and in the meantime you get to use your savings to pay off some of your smaller debts. In a nutshell, your money is working for you. Then once you are debt-free, you will be able to save more than you ever thought possible.

So you say you'd love to dip into savings to pay off your debt but the savings cupboard is bare! Don't be discouraged. You are simply like most of the other people on your block. Continue following the debt elimination plan outlined in this chapter. We will discuss setting up an aggressive yet workable savings plan in Chapter Ten.

When A Debt Is Eliminated

Each time a Target Debt is paid off, draw a line through it with a highlighting pen. Don't erase it from your Debt Elimination Schedule; just set it off from the others. The next debt on the list then becomes your new Target Debt, and all of your energies should focus on it. (Don't forget, debts should be listed in order of their current balance, from smallest to largest).

Plan A
Using the TARGET Software

The debt elimination process outlined in Plan A is amazing! The beauty of it is that it is completely accurate and the computer does all the math. In fact, one of the more popular features of the TARGET program is the Debt Elimination Schedule.

After you run the program you may want to copy the information from your computer DES over to the DES in this book, or print it out for your folder, for easy, "at-a-glance" reference.

The TARGET computer program has been designed with a basic computer set-up in mind. The specific hardware requirements and documentation for running the program are included with the software. TARGET is also extremely easy to learn and use—even if you've never used a computer before. If you don't have an IBM compatible personal computer, borrow a friend's for an hour or so. You might even be able to stay late at work one night and use the boss's. And as was mentioned earlier, local colleges and libraries also have computers available to the general public.

If you decide not to use the TARGET software program, you have two options. *D.C. Publishers & Management* will generate your DES for you, or you can do it by hand. If you choose the first option, you will have to provide *D.C. Publishers* with all the necessary information: name of creditor, date loan was taken out, interest rate, monthly payment, balance, etc. *D.C. Publishers* can also provide you with amortization schedules for any of your loans. Information on this service can be found in Appendix D. Appendix D also has details on ordering the TARGET personal finance software if you did not purchase it when you bought this book.

If you decide to do your DES by hand, a small, inexpensive calculator will be a big help. Completing your DES by hand is very easy; however, due to interest calculations, keep in mind that your figures will not be 100% accurate.

Nonetheless, you should be able to come very close to projecting an exact date as to when you will be totally debt free.

Plan B
Without the TARGET Software

If you are doing your DES by hand, you will now need to fill in the remaining columns on your Debt Elimination Schedule. The "Accrued Payment" of the first bill on the list is the same as its monthly payment.

To figure the accrued payment of each bill thereafter, simply add the *monthly* payment of the bill in question to the *accrued* payment of the bill prior.

Just to be sure you've got it, look over the following example. The accrued payment of the first bill on the list is the same as the monthly payment.

To figure the second bill's accrued payment, add its monthly payment to the accrued payment of the first bill.

The table below shows a sample Debt Elimination Schedule. The number we are currently figuring is in bold print.

	Creditor/Lender	Original Balance	DES Start Date	Current Balance	Monthly Payment	Payoff Balance	Accrued Payment	Projected Payoff
1	JCPenney	$ 475.00	2/01/93	$ 45.00	$ 20.00		$ 20.00	
2	Jewelry Ltd.	350.00	2/01/93	125.00	25.00		**45.00**	
3	Carpet Country	1,200.00	2/01/93	313.09				
4								

1. Monthly payment for debt #2, $25.00.
2. "Accrued Payment" of previous bill, $20.00.
3. $25 + $20 = $45.
4. "Accrued Payment" for debt #2 is $45.00.

Now go ahead and calculate the "Accrued Payment" for the third debt on the sample provided.

	Creditor/Lender	Original Balance	DES Start Date	Current Balance	Monthly Payment	Payoff Balance	Accrued Payment	Projected Payoff
1	JCPenney	$ 475.00	2/01/93	$ 45.00	$ 20.00		$ 20.00	
2	Jewelry Ltd.	350.00	2/01/93	125.00	25.00		45.00	
3	Carpet Country	1,200.00	2/01/93	313.09	54.39		**99.39**	
4								

You should have come up with an "Accrued Payment" for Carpet Country of $99.39 ($45.00 + $54.39 = $99.39)

Now go back and calculate the accrued payment for each of the debts on your own DES. Notice that the accrued payment gets larger as you move down the list.

Remember, it is the accrued payment of the Target Debt (the debt you are focusing on) that you will send to the creditor each month. Do not, I repeat, DO NOT, pay more than the minimum amount due on any bill other than your Target Debt.

By the same token, don't get so caught up in your Target Debt that you forget to make the regular monthly payments on your other bills. If you do, you will destroy your credit rating and create trouble with your creditors.

Also notice that even though the accrued payment keeps getting larger, the amount out of pocket each month stays the same. The reason, of course, is because debts are being eliminated and their old monthly payments are being added to the accrued payment of the next debt on the list.

Once your accrued payments have been filled in, you are now ready to compute the "Payoff Balances" and "Projected Payoffs" associated with each of your debts.

The payoff balance for the first debt will be the same as the current balance. This is the amount needed to pay off the debt or to eliminate it. Make sure this is reflected on your own DES.

Now, to determine the projected payoff date, divide debt number one's payoff balance by its accrued payment and round the result **up** to the nearest whole number.

For example (see chart at top of next page), let's say JCPenney is the first debt on the list. The payoff balance is $45 and the accrued payment is $20. Thus 45 ÷ 20 = 2.25 (This is where your calculator comes in handy.) Round 2.25 up to 3. Always round up! (You'll understand why later in the chapter.) This is the number of months it will take to pay off this debt. Thus, if you begin this plan in February of 1993, JCPenney would be paid off three months later with the April payment.

	Creditor/Lender	Original Balance	DES Start Date	Current Balance	Monthly Payment	Payoff Balance	Accrued Payment	Projected Payoff
1	JCPenney	$ 475.00	2/01/93	$ 45.00	$ 20.00	$ 45.00	$ 20.00	**4/01/93**
2	Jewelry Ltd.	350.00	2/01/93	125.00	25.00		45.00	
3	Carpet Country	1,200.00	2/01/93	313.09				
4								

1. $45 divided by $20 = 2.25 months.
2. Round 2.25 months up to 3 months
3. The projected payoff date is three months away, or April of 1993.

You can now compute the payoff balances and projected payoff dates of all the remaining debts.

In our example, between February and April (the date you paid off the first bill), you were making regular monthly payments of $25 to Jewelry Ltd., right? Right! So in May, when Jewelry Ltd. becomes your Target Debt, its payoff balance will only be $50. See the following example.

	Creditor/Lender	Original Balance	DES Start Date	Current Balance	Monthly Payment	Payoff Balance	Accrued Payment	Projected Payoff
1	JCPenney	$ 475.00	2/01/93	$ 45.00	$ 20.00	$ 45.00	$ 20.00	4/01/93
2	Jewelry Ltd.	350.00	2/01/93	125.00	25.00	**50.00**	45.00	
3	Carpet Country	1,200.00	2/01/93	313.09				
4								

1. 3 monthly payments made to Jewelry Ltd. between Feb. 1993 and April 1993 at $25.00 each = $75.00
2. That $75.00 subtracted from the $125.00 Current Balance = $50.00
3. Thus $50.00 will be the new Payoff Balance in May, when Jewelry Ltd. becomes your Target Debt.

You can now take the payoff balance of Jewelry Ltd. and divide it by its accrued payment and, voila, you have the number of months before it is paid off as well. From there, you can determine its projected payoff date.

	Creditor/Lender	Original Balance	DES Start Date	Current Balance	Monthly Payment	Payoff Balance	Accrued Payment	Projected Payoff
1	JCPenney	$ 475.00	2/01/93	$ 45.00	$ 20.00	$ 45.00	$ 20.00	4/01/93
2	Jewelry Ltd.	350.00	2/01/93	125.00	25.00	50.00	45.00	**6/01/93**
3	Carpet Country	1,200.00	2/01/93	313.09	54.39		99.39	
4								

1. $50.00 payoff amount divided by $45.00 accrued payment = 1.11 months.
2. Round 1.11 months up to 2 months.
3. Thus the projected payoff date for Jewelry Ltd. will be <u>two</u> <u>months</u> beyond the payoff date of the previous bill, or in this case, June.

The cycle continues. Now use the projected payoff date of the second debt to determine how many payments you will have paid on the third debt since beginning the plan. Then figure the payoff balance and the projected payoff date for the third debt. If you do this correctly you should come up with $95.53 as the payoff balance and 7/1/93 as the projected payoff date.

1. Four payments at $54.39 = $217.56
2. $313.09 current balance minus $217.56 = $95.53 (payoff balance)
3. $95.53 divided by $99.39 (accrued payment) = 0.96 months
4. 0.96 months rounded up to 1 month.
5. Projected payoff date is July 1993.

By the way, be aware that because you are making regular monthly payments on all your other debts, some of them will already be paid off before they have a chance to become the Target Debt. Don't let this throw you off. Just apply the monthly payment you have been making on it to the accrued payment of your current Target Debt.

For example (see chart at top of next page), let's suppose the fourth bill on the list is XYZ Furniture. By the time it becomes your Target Debt, its regular monthly payments will have already paid it off. Thus, its payoff balance will be zero! When this happens, apply the amount of XYZ's monthly payment ($66.89) to the accrued payment of the next Target Debt.

	Creditor/Lender	Original Balance	DES Start Date	Current Balance	Monthly Payment	Payoff Balance	Accrued Payment	Projected Payoff
1	JCPenney	$ 475.00	2/01/93	$ 45.00	$ 20.00	$ 45.00	$ 20.00	4/01/93
2	Jewelry Ltd.	350.00	2/01/93	125.00	25.00	50.00	45.00	6/01/93
3	Carpet Country	1,200.00	2/01/93	313.09	54.39	95.53	99.39	7/01/93
4	XYZ Furniture	525.00	2/01/93	340.00	66.89	0.00	166.25	7/01/93
5	Sam's Computer	2,300.00	2/01/93	699.00	79.00	304.00	245.25	8/01/93

Pretty simple, right? Before you know it, you will be totally debt free! Your accrued payments get larger and larger and your debts are eliminated faster and faster. And you are not increasing the amount of money out of your pocket by one cent! Best of all, you know exactly what is going on at all times. You are in control. You can look at the last bill on the list at any time and know exactly when you will be 100% debt free!

A Word About Interest For Those Not Using the TARGET Software

Wait a minute, you cry! What about all the interest I'm paying! Doesn't that affect the amount that is actually being paid on each bill? Won't that throw off my payoff balances, my payoff dates and my accrued payments? The answer to that question is, yes. That is the price paid when you figure your DES by hand. But not to worry. That is also the reason you round **up** when figuring payoff dates.

The number of months you gain when you round up on each bill will help offset the amount you will be losing in interest

payments. The only time this will not be true is when your bills are in the thousands of dollars. Then, of course, you will be paying a larger amount toward the interest, and it will take a bit longer to eliminate the debt.

In order to accurately take into account the interest being paid on these larger debts, you will have to refigure and reevaluate your DES every other month or so. And even then, be aware that your totals and dates will not be 100% accurate. But they will be very close.

Okay, What Do I Do Now?

Don't stop! With the instructions and steps outlined up to this point, accompanied with some patience and self-control, there is no reason why you cannot be totally debt free in a relatively short amount of time. Once you are debt free, and even before, you can use the information found in the next chapter to cut years off of your home mortgage loan and save tens of thousands of dollars in interest.

Of course, it is only reasonable to assume that emergencies or unexpected expenses will arise as you are following this plan. Again, be flexible, and don't get an ulcer if you need to readjust your goals by a month or two. The key is to be consistent. With the computer program by your side, if you find yourself making an unforseen purchase two months from now, all you have to do is go into the program and create the new debt. Then run a new Debt Elimination Schedule to come up with a new date for being debt free. If you are not using the computer program, all you have to do is follow the instructions for Plan B, copy a DES from the appendix, then add your new debt to the list, and recalculate.

And Once I'm Debt Free?

You do not need me to tell you what to do with your money once you are debt free. What I will say, however, is to be sure you follow "The Spending Plan" that will be explained in Chapter Nine. If you do, you should be able to continually improve your credit profile and credit standing without going further into debt.

"The Spending Plan" will also be much more enjoyable once you're debt free because you will have so much more to spend!

That's right. Once you are debt free, the amount at the bottom of the Monthly Payment column on your DES is yours free and clear, each and every month, to do with as you please. Also, once you are debt free, you will be able to follow these same debt reducing principles to help you do other things: to help you save more than you ever thought possible (establishing a savings plan is discussed in

Chapter Ten), to travel to the places most people don't even dare to dream about, and to keep a balance of thousands of dollars in your checkbook at all times!

A Word About Consolidation Loans

At one time considered the greatest debt elimination tool ever invented, consolidation loans have proven to be anything but that. Consolidation loans are loans that pay off all of your smaller debts and loans. Then you only have the one payment on the larger loan, often at a lower interest rate and lower monthly payment than you were making on all the others combined.

Seems like a great idea? Well, for some it is. For others it is nothing less than total disaster. You see, most people just do not have the self-control to make a consolidation loan work.

As soon as the loan comes through and all of their debts are "paid off," so to speak, they find some "good" reason to charge just this one last time. Before they know it, they not only have the big consolidation loan to pay off, but all those little debts are back again as well. Instead of consolidating their payments, they have doubled them!

A former neighbor asked me about consolidation loans. He was convinced that he could handle one and that he had the self-control to make it work. (Anyone substantially in debt should probably face the fact that financial self-control is not one of their strong points.) Because he didn't want to get another loan from a

"Have you considered consolidating your medication?
Lots of little pills into one big pill."

bank, he decided to give himself a consolidation loan by taking a cash advance off one of his credit cards.

The sad thing is that it could have worked. He used the money to pay off all of his smaller credit, charge, and department store cards. He paid off virtually every creditor he owed money to.

Less than a week later, he decided he had done so well and was so smart that he should go out and celebrate. He took his wife out for a night on the town—a nice dinner and shopping. They didn't spend a lot. They bought the baby two new dresses. After all, the department store charge card was "free and clear" so they could afford to charge a little something.

They could pay it off as soon as the bill came, right?

Then when the weekend rolled around they decided to go skiing. It had been so long since they could afford to do things like that, and, after all, there was fresh powder on the slopes.

Today, they have three children, a huge consolidation loan and all the same debt that their consolidation loan had originally paid off.

The principle behind consolidation loans is a good one. Some people have gotten them and have done exactly what they set out to do. But the vast majority only find themselves with twice the debt.

If you decide to go this route, you should do two things first.

1. Make sure you have the determination and self-control necessary to make the system work.

2. Re-read this chapter. You may find that a consolidation loan is not as easy to manage as it first appears.

Bankruptcy, Better Known As The Ten Year Mistake

This is as good a place as any to explain the good and bad associated with filing bankruptcy. To begin with, you need to understand that I am a bit biased when it comes to bankruptcy. I feel strongly that if *you* got yourself into the situation you're in, then *you* can get yourself out.

As we have discussed throughout this chapter, there <u>are</u> other alternatives to debt elimination besides filing bankruptcy. Besides bankruptcy can, and most likely will, show up on your credit report for ten years after filing. Despite the come-ons in your local classified section, there is no miracle formula to getting out of debt. And as many have found out, bankruptcy may just be the debt-elimination plan from hell.

But before you let me totally destroy your hopes of bankruptcy as an alternative, understand that it does exist, it is legal, and it is also relatively easy to file. Millions have filed in the past, and millions will file in the future. It is your legal right to gain relief from your debts in this manner. The only problem is that what is legal may not always be what is best. Read through the steps outlined in this book. It may take a little longer for you to gain relief by following this plan than by filing bankruptcy, but I guarantee you will feel better about yourself and your future will be much brighter if you work things out on your own. Nonetheless, there are those who find themselves in so deep that there may be no other alternative.

Whatever you do, don't let anyone tell you that a certain dollar figure justifies bankruptcy. Regardless of your income or lack of income, being $1,000, $100,000 or $100,000,000 in debt does not mean bankruptcy is your best option. There are plenty of people who have successfully conquered hundreds of thousands of dollars in debt without filing with the bankruptcy court.

This book outlines what I consider to be the best debt elimination plan found anywhere. But if, after reading through this entire text, you still feel that bankruptcy is for you, you have that right. Whatever the case, you may want to consider the following points before you make your decision.

*   The emotional side of filing bankruptcy should be seriously considered, as it often can do more harm than the good that comes out of being relieved of your debts.

*   Filing bankruptcy does not mean you get to keep everything you have purchased without paying for it. Often, everything you have can be taken to satisfy your debts. It all depends on whether your property is exempt or

non-exempt. You may find it better to get rid of the things you cannot afford, keep the things you need or want, and find a way to pay for them.

- Under Chapter 7 Bankruptcy, your assets will be sold in order to satisfy your debts.

- All of your debts may not be eliminated by filing bankruptcy. If you find that the bulk of your debt is non-dischargeable, bankruptcy is probably not the best solution for you. Non-dischargeable debts include child support, alimony, most student loans, state and federal income taxes, fines resulting from legal action or traffic offenses, and many more.

- Bankruptcy only protects you. If a friend or family member has co-signed with you on a purchase or a loan, the creditor can, and will, go after them if you file for bankruptcy.

Not knowing your exact situation, I cannot tell you whether bankruptcy is right or wrong for you. Bankruptcy, for the most part, is a more viable option for businesses than it is for individuals. But if after studying your own situation you still feel bankruptcy is the answer, see an attorney. You can find one in any phone book or in the classified section of a newspaper under "Personals," "Debt," "Attorneys," "Lawyers," or "Bankruptcy." Some lawyers even specialize in bankruptcy. They will likely have the best grasp on the current laws for your state. If you do seek the advice of a lawyer, be sure to go to one who will give you the initial consultation for free. Take a list of

your debts and assets with you and see what he or she has to say. Be sure to go in prepared because the second visit will cost you! Another thing to keep in mind is that attorneys make their money off of people like you. Chances are the lawyer will be in favor of you filing bankruptcy. It doesn't affect *their* credit, and *they* make money in the deal. Analyze the pros and cons of bankruptcy very carefully.

The Wage Earner Plan

If you are going to file bankruptcy, file the one that is going to do the least amount of damage to your personal well-being and your current standard of living. Commonly referred to as Chapter 13, the Wage Earner Plan may be what you are looking for.

Keep in mind that I strongly recommend following the debt elimination plan outlined in this chapter first and would suggest bankruptcy, in any form, only as an extreme last resort.

Although Chapter 13, or the Wage Earner Plan, is a form of bankruptcy and is filed with the bankruptcy court, it is less intimidating than the harsher bankruptcies and achieves similar results.

The major difference between Chapter 13 and other forms of bankruptcy is that with Chapter 13, you still repay all of your debts. The courts, however, make it much easier for you to pay them than it might otherwise be. Although laws vary from state to state, the following list should help to identify some of the benefits of filing Chapter 13.

- You escape having several negative marks on your credit report from non-payment of debts.

- Creditors are forbidden by law to contact you or harass you after your papers are filed with the court.

- Your debts are frozen where they are from the minute you file. No further late charges or interest charges can be applied to your debt load.

- No more garnishment of wages or salary can be initiated by your creditors or employer.

- Favorable repayment schedules are almost always extended to help you meet your obligations.

- The courts often let you set up your own repayment schedule if your plan is within reason.

- You are not refused the right to reestablish your credit worthiness or obtain new credit while you are on the Wage Earner Plan.

- Once your papers are filed, the laws in most states protect you from repossessions, foreclosures, and evictions.

- You are allowed to keep your property while you attempt to repay your debts, usually over a three- to five-year period.

- The process is relatively easy and with the forms available at the U.S. District Courts in your area, the Wage Earner Plan can usually be handled without the added expense of hiring an attorney.

As this is only a partial listing of what Chapter 13 Bankruptcy does and does not do, it will be necessary to get the proper papers, perhaps talk to an attorney with expertise in bankruptcy, or, at the very least, check with your local library for information on bankruptcy.

But even still, as you will learn in Chapter Six, most of the things accomplished through Chapter 13 Bankruptcy can usually be accomplished by yourself through direct negotiations with your creditors. It is best to try every other alternative before filing bankruptcy.

Chapter Four

Cutting Your Mortgage In Half

There is nothing permanent except change.
- Heraclitus

Have you ever dreamed about owning a $100,000 home, a $500,000 home, or maybe even a $1,000,000 home? Well, you may not be that far away from your goal. In fact, you may already be there.

You see, the average home, with a price tag of $85,000 at 10.5% interest on a 30-year mortgage, will actually end up costing you $280,516! That's right, total interest and principal combined is over $280,000. That's over three times the value of the home. You could have purchased three of these homes for the price of the one by the time you are through making your payments.

Can this be right? Yes! Is it fair? Not by a long shot! But what can you do about it? Well, your banker will probably tell you there is nothing you can do about it. Believe me, your banker is wrong. There are ways that you can legally fight back without it costing you any more of your hard earned money.

Yes, there will always be interest, unless of course your rich aunt leaves you enough to pay cash for the home. But with the right information, that interest can be cut down to a bare minimum, saving you tens of thousands, and possibly hundreds of thousands of dollars in the meantime.

The information contained in this chapter, like the information contained in the previous chapters, amounts to nothing more than a logically thought-out formula for accomplishing the task at hand—eliminating your debts or, in this case, your home mortgage loan.

You have undoubtedly seen programs advertised in newspapers and magazines purporting to slash your mortgage in half or pay off your entire mortgage in a fraction of the time remaining on your loan. Many of these programs sell for $50, $100 and more. And even though a program that could save you thousands of dollars on your mortgage would be worth such an investment, you do not need to buy these special courses to do this. If you own your own home, or are thinking about purchasing your own home, the information in the following pages should be of great help.

Amortization Schedules

There are actually a few different ways to cut your mortgage payments and save thousands of dollars in the meantime. But before you can follow any of these plans, you need to know what the current interest-to-principal ratio on your mortgage is. You will need an amortization schedule to determine this.

An amortization schedule is nothing more than a balance sheet broken down over the course of your loan. It is set up to project the payment due each month, how much of that payment will be applied toward the interest, how much to the principal, and, finally, what the balance due will be at the end of any given month over the course of the loan.

As was explained earlier, the Till Debt Due Us Part TARGET computer program is already set up to generate amortization schedules for you. If you do not have the TARGET software you can get an amortization schedule from your bank (usually for a modest fee) or *D.C. Publishers & Management* can generate your amortization schedules for you. (See Appendix D.)

Once you have your amortization schedule, look at the current month's payment. How much of it is going to the principal? How much to the interest? Surprised? Most people are not only surprised but are almost physically ill when they discover how little is actually going toward the principal each month. When will the loan be paid off? Does it seem like an eternity? It doesn't have to be.

By following the debt elimination program outlined in the previous chapter, you will already be cutting years off the length of your loan. When all of your other debts are paid off and your home mortgage becomes your Target Debt, its accrued payment should be quite high.

That is the key to paying off your mortgage early; paying more toward the principal than the interest each month. By following the debt elimination plan, you will automatically save tens of thousands of dollars in interest on your home mortgage and will be totally debt free in a relatively short period of time.

"But," you say, "once I pay off all of my debts and have nothing left but my mortgage, I want to begin using some of that money to play and relax, not to pay on my mortgage."

No problem! Start using *most* of your new found wealth to save, invest, travel, or just to pay cash for the finer things in life, but keep out just enough money to *double* your monthly mortgage payment.

"Are you crazy? Doubling my payment will use up every penny of my new found wealth!"

Actually, doubling your payment is easier than you think and a heck of a lot cheaper. Here's how it works. Doubling a $750 payment does not mean paying $1500. You do not need to double the entire amount, only the amount going to the <u>principal</u>. After all, the principal is the only part of your payment that is actually going toward paying off the loan. The interest portion of the payment is going into your banker's pocket.

For example, if you are currently paying $750 a month toward your mortgage and your amortization schedule reveals that only $125 of that payment is going toward the principal this month, all you have to do is pay another $125 dollars a month for a total of $875. That $875 payment will, in essence, apply the same amount to the principal as would two consecutive regular monthly payments totaling $1500. Doubling your principal payment in this manner saves you an immediate $625 in interest.

You will also notice when looking at your amortization schedule that, as time passes, the amount going to the principal increases. It is not necessary to continually double this amount each time it goes up. Of course, if you do you will pay off the mortgage much sooner and save even more, but this may not be realistic,

considering the fact that you want to use some of your freed-up monies on yourself and your family. Instead, just commit a certain amount of money that you will apply toward the principal each month and stick with it. It doesn't have to be $500 or even $100. Twenty-five additional dollars paid each month will still save you thousands of dollars in interest and cut years off your loan.

If you decide to use the TARGET computer software, run two or three different amortization schedules with different monthly payments. Then decide which monthly payment will be realistic and best for you. You'll be amazed at what an extra $25, $50, or $100 will do.

Buying Equity

By following this plan you are not actually spending more each month; rather, you are opening up a new savings account of sorts.

You see, every penny that you apply toward the principal of your home mortgage loan is actually building up your equity. Thus, in addition to the tens of thousands of dollars you are saving in interest, you will also get back every penny you've applied to the principal, if and when, you sell the home. (Assuming the actual value of your home is not decreasing.) Now doesn't this make more sense than putting that $25, $50 or $100 dollars a month into a regular savings account at 5¼% interest? Think about it—it's not costing you anything at all because you're getting it all back in equity and interest savings!

But I Can't Pay Any More Than I Already Am

Even if you think you're maxed out with what you are already paying, go ahead and run an amortization schedule anyway. Figure an extra $25 a month or so added onto your monthly payment. Once you see how many years you will cut off your loan and how many thousands of dollars you will be saving, I think you will find the extra $25!

Okay, you've done that and you still cannot come up with the extra money. There is an alternative. You can still slash your monthly payments and save tens of thousands of dollars without spending anymore money out of pocket. This plan allows you to pay your normal monthly payment, but on an altered payment schedule. Instead of paying your payment once a month, you will need to divide it in half and pay the smaller amount every two weeks.

For example, if you are currently paying $750 per month, you will need to divide that amount in two and pay $375 every two weeks. This payment schedule actually makes more sense in today's world because so many people are getting their paychecks biweekly. As you can see, it doesn't cost anymore each month, but you do have to write out two separate checks.

"How," you may ask, "does this reduce my payments?" Well, it is actually quite simple. By making your payments every two weeks, at the end of the year you will have made 26 bi-weekly payments (equal to 13 regular payments). That "extra payment" is applied directly to the principal of your loan. By doing this the interest you pay is slashed little by little down to zero!

Be sure to check with your banker to see if this type of payment schedule is acceptable with your particular loan. Many banks, in fact, are now offering the bi-weekly payment schedule as an option when they write new loans.

Let's look at a working example. Joe holds an $85,000 mortgage on his home. His payments are $746 a month at 10% interest for 30 years. Twelve monthly payments at $746 each equals $8,952. But by making $373 payments every two weeks, he will make 26 payments totalling $9,698, a difference of $746 (one extra payment). That $746 applied toward the principal each and every year will slash 10 years off of Joe's mortgage and save him more than $64,000 in interest. Another important point is that Joe is building equity at almost triple the rate compared to making regular once-a-month payments.

Let's look at a couple of other examples.

A $90,000 mortgage at 8.5% interest would amount to this:

Term of Loan	Payment	Years to Payoff	Total Interest Paid
30 yr. fixed	$692.00	30 yrs.	$159,156.80
30 yr. bi-weekly	$346.00	22 yrs. 5 mo.	$111,377.72

A $100,000 mortgage at 10.5% interest would amount to this:

Term of Loan	Payment	Years to Payoff	Total Interest Paid
30 yr. fixed	$914.00	30 yrs.	$230,925.56
30 yr. bi-weekly	$457.00	20 yrs. 6 mo.	$143,958.46

The TARGET personal finance computer software will automatically calculate bi-weekly payments on your amortization schedule for any of your loans.

This plan will also work with other types of consumer debts: car loans, boat loans, student loans, home improvement loans, or personal loans.

By paying the same amount out of pocket each month, but altering the payment schedule, you save tens of thousands of dollars and cut ten years, or more, off the length of your loan. And the best part of all is you can begin putting this plan into action today. But you must realize, like every other plan outlined in this book, the key to success is you. Only you can make this work.

And isn't the inconvenience of writing two checks instead of one worth it? Should you decide to try the bi-weekly payment plan but find your banker won't

"No, YOU pay the interest. Your grandchildren pay the principal."

allow it, there is still a way to make it work. Remember, the key to the bi-weekly system is that by the end of the year you will have made one extra full payment toward the principal on the loan. If your bank tells you they don't allow bi-weekly payments, just divide your regular payment by twelve and pay the amount you come up with (the number you get when you divide your payment by twelve) as an additional principal payment each month. Your payment coupon/stub should have a line or box where you can indicate an extra amount to be applied to principal.

Let's look at an example. If your regular monthly payment is $789, divide that payment by twelve (twelve months).

$$789 \div 12 = 65.75$$

Now, according to this example, all you need to do is pay an extra $65.75 each month and indicate on your payment coupon/stub that you want that extra amount applied toward the principal on your loan. By doing this you achieve the same results as you would by following the bi-weekly payment plan. And, best of all, your banker has no choice but to accept your money.

If you decide not to follow this payment option, it is still a good idea to add an additional amount to the principal on your loan payments whenever possible. In fact, this is probably the safest investment available today. After all, there isn't a broker or financial advisor alive who will watch and take care of your investment portfolio the way you will watch and take care of your own home!

Now that you are getting excited or at least interested in paying off your home,

you should be aware that there is a down side to being mortgage free. Yes, you will be relieved of having to come up with that hefty payment each and every month, year after year. But you will also give up one of the last tax deductions available: the interest on your home mortgage.

For most of us, though, being *totally* debt free is a pretty good trade-off. Then once you are debt and mortgage free, you can use your money to buy other real estate, rental properties, etc., if you still need the tax write-off. A good tax or investment advisor can show you several lucrative options that will put your freed-up money in your pocket instead of in Uncle Sam's.

The Rush To Refinance!

Some argue that it was a post Gulf War or post recession economic recovery. Others argue that it was the "Fed" and election year politics playing games with the consumer again. Whatever it was, 1992 and 1993 saw homeowners rushing to refinance their home mortgages in record numbers. Not since the mid-'70s had interest rates been this low. Why refinance? To save money, of course, and pay off your loan sooner.

Let's examine this one a little closer. A homeowner with a $100,000 mortgage at 30 years and 10.5% interest would have a monthly payment of about $915. That same loan refinanced at 8% would have monthly payments of only $734 per month; a savings of over $180 per month. If, however, this homeowner wanted to refinance but continue paying the higher payment each month, he or she could actually pay off the home in about 16 years, or just over half the time of the original loan.

Of course, when you refinance, you have to take into consideration the time you have been paying on your current loan.

For example, if you have a 30 year mortgage and you have been paying on it for six years, refinancing the loan into another 30 year mortgage will mean that you will actually be paying for your home for thirty-six years.

Other factors to take into consideration: How much lower of an interest rate can you get? Most real estate analysts agree that if you can shave two to three points or more off your interest rate, refinancing is a good idea. There is a catch however. To really make it worth your while, you will have to stay in your home at least long enough to recoup the money you pay in points and other closing costs. (See chart on page 50.)

A point equals one percent of the loan amount. Thus, one point on a $94,000 home would be $940. Most loans carry with them other closing fees as well: a loan origination fee of one percent, title insurance, appraisal fees, etc.

You can count on points and fees running from three to five percent of the amount refinanced on a typical loan. So for a $94,000 loan, you could count on closing costs ranging anywhere from $2,820 to $4,700 dollars. Occasionally, banks will let you negotiate a no-point loan for a higher interest rate as well.

Another factor to keep in mind when refinancing is the current market value of

your home. Many parts of the country actually saw a sharp decrease in property values in the late 1980s and early 1990s and most lenders will only refinance at 80% of the value of your home. So if your home has decreased in value, you will probably find that you do not qualify for a new loan unless you have a substantial cash down payment.

The worksheet on the following page will help you determine approximately how much you will pay in closing costs if you are refinancing or purchasing a new home, and show you how long it will take for you to "recoup" the fees, or break even, on the closing costs associated with refinancing.

The chart on page 50 includes an example loan for $125,000. *Other than discount points, which are a percentage of the loan total, the fee amounts listed are a pretty safe average nationwide.*

Obviously, buying, selling, or refinancing a home is not something you should jump into without first doing your homework. Second only to getting out of debt, a real estate transaction could prove to be one of the smartest financial moves you'll make. One mistake, however, and it could take years to recover.

There is a Glossary of some of the most commonly referred to real estate and finance terms at the end of this book. Study them well. If you find that you are still not comfortable with the financial jargon; find a competent real estate agent or financial advisor to help you along. The commissions or fees you'll pay will be well worth it.

Estimated Closing Costs   **Example**   **Your Home**

1. Loan Origination Fee (1%) . . . . . . $1,250.00 $ _____
2. Loan discount points (variable) . . . . 1,875.00 (1½%)   _____
3. Appraisal Fee . . . . 250.00   _____
4. Credit Report . . . . 50.00   _____
5. Title Search and Insurance . . . . 500.00   _____
6. Endorsements to title policy . . . . 35.00   _____
7. Recording Fees . . . . 50.00   _____
8. Application Fee . . . . 50.00   _____
9. Lender's Underwriting Fee . . . . 200.00   _____
10. Transfer taxes . . . . 1,250.00   _____
11. Other . . . . 0.00   _____

Total closing costs . . . . $5,510.00 $ _____

The Break Even Point On Refinancing

1. Monthly mortgage payment . . . . $1,190.00   _____
    before refinancing
    (Principal and Interest only)
    (i.e., 125K mortgage
    for 30 years at 11%)

2. Subtract the principal-and
    interest-only monthly payments
    on the new mortgage.
    (i.e., 125K mortgage for
    30 years at 8.5%) . . . . -961.00   - _____

3. The result is your pre-tax . . . . =229.00   = _____
    savings each month.

4. Multiply your tax-rate (i.e., 31%)
    by the pre-tax savings above, and subtract
    the result. (Tax-rates are listed on
    the following page.) . . . . -71.00   - _____

5. This is your after-tax savings . . . . =158.00   = _____
    per month.

6. Divide the total cost of . . . . 34.87 months   _____
    refinancing ($5,510) by your
    after-tax savings per month ($158)

It will take approximately 35 months to break even on the closing costs associated with the refinanced loan in our example.

Tax Rate Schedules

Caution: *These tax rates are for illustrative purposes only and should not be used when filing your Federal Income Taxes.*

Single filing status

If your taxable income is Over—	But not Over—	Your tax rate is—
$ 0	$ 21,450	15%
21,450	51,900	28%
51,900	--------	31%

Married filing jointly filing status

If your taxable income is Over—	But not Over—	Your tax rate is—
$ 0	$ 35,800	15%
35,800	86,500	28%
86,500	--------	31%

Married filing separately filing status

If your taxable income is Over—	But not Over—	Your tax rate is—
$ 0	$ 17,900	15%
17,900	43,250	28%
43,250	--------	31%

Head of Household filing status

If your taxable income is Over—	But not Over—	Your tax rate is—
$ 0	$ 28,750	15%
28,750	74,150	28%
74,150	--------	31%

Chapter Five

Turning Your World Around

Even if you're on the right track, you'll
get run over if you just sit there.
- Will Rogers

If at times you feel not only like turning your world around but upside down and inside out as well, trying to find out where everything went wrong, don't despair. There are countless others in the same situation. Somehow you got in over your head. Just remember, things are not as bad as they might seem. You owe some money, and that is all.

Don't let your financial situation dictate how you are going to feel about life or how you are going to live it today or tomorrow. Yesterday is behind you. There is no reason to look back, unless it is to say, "I learned my lesson." That lesson may have been an expensive one, but you can make sure that you don't have to learn it again. The preceding chapters

in this book teach you everything from setting up realistic goals to slashing your home mortgage. They deal with practice, patience and perseverance. This chapter, on the other hand, deals with the rest of the formula for success—deciding what is and isn't necessary and what sacrifices you can comfortably make as you implement your debt elimination program.

The advice and counsel given in this chapter is just that: advice and counsel. *You* will have to decide where you fall in the spectrum of life and what in this chapter applies to you. You may find that none of it applies. If that is the case, move on! But if you find that something here does apply, take a deep breath and do what has to be done. You are not the first,

"Yes I am a kindergarten teacher. But I've had to take a second job
as a Bounty Hunter."

nor will you be the last, to be in your current situation. But you *are* the one who will determine how long you will stay in that situation. The key to getting through the rough times in life is to remember that situations are only temporary. You can effect positive change; all you need is the desire and/or willingness to change, and the rest will fall into place.

This chapter will deal with everything from finding the appropriate second job to buying the right insurance policy. Again, some of this may apply, some of it may not. The key is to read through it and see. If it doesn't apply, the added knowledge may help you help somebody else.

It's Off To Work We Go

One of the harsh realities of life is that most of us will have to work for a living. Another of the harsh realities is that if our

jobs do not pay enough to live on, we should probably be looking around. I'm not advocating quitting your job because you want more money. What I am advocating is determining whether you are making enough to meet your obligations. If you are not, you have two choices: find a way to make more money or get rid of some of your obligations.

Let's pursue the "more money" idea for a minute. Depending on the amount of debt you have, you may want to consider supplementing your income with a second job. Sure, you could always go out and find a higher paying job, but for most people this will not seem like a realistic option. If you have the time, go for it. But if you are like most other Americans, you may want to keep the job you have and get a second, part-time job. At least this way, you will have the income needed to survive while you are looking for that higher paying position.

Weekend work is great. A couple of evenings a week are fine, or maybe an early morning paper route. If your spouse or kids are not working, they may need to get part-time work as well. Swallow some pride. It will pay off in the long-run. The key is to remember that all of this is temporary. You are not the first to have to do this, nor will you be the last. But if you do it right the first time, you won't have to do it again.

Where do you find these jobs? Friends, family, and neighbors are good sources to check with. The classified ads are also a good place to start. Make a promise to yourself that you will take a job this week, or at least that you will apply for a job listed in this week's paper. Then just do it! Don't take a door-to-door or a get-rich-quick job. Get a real job, something with a firm base and a solid reputation. McDonald's is a good choice. The mall is always hiring. Remember, this is not a career change, it's extra income! Be aware, however, that you may find you like this second job so much more than your first that you end up changing over to full-time.

You should also note that with part-time work you may have to settle for lower wages than you are accustomed to. Minimum wage or slightly higher may have to suffice. Other possible job options are typing term papers at home for students, baby sitting, cleaning houses, etc. If you are willing to work, the work is out there waiting for you. Whatever you do, the extra income will go a long way toward making life's burdens easier to bear.

I Don't Want A Second Job!

If you don't want a second job, don't get a second job. There are other ways to accomplish the task at hand besides coming up with ways to increase your income. The best way, of course, is to decrease your expenses.

How do you do this? First of all, set up a budget. You need to know how much you have coming in each month and how much you have going out each month. Then determine which monthly expenses can be eliminated.

For most, probably the easiest thing to eliminate will be dining out. When my wife and I first got married, we were eating out every night of the week. After spending our days at work and school, neither of us felt up to cooking dinner. On average we spent $15 per day on fast food. That is $105 a week. We barely made that much money! Then we set a goal to not eat out for a day, then a week, and then a month. We did it. We went grocery shopping. And this time, instead of buying chips and salsa, we bought ground beef and chicken. We also bought instant potatoes, gravy mix, canned vegetables, spaghetti sauce, and frozen pizzas. It was amazing; nothing that we couldn't just open, heat and serve, but still good food at a great price.

We made it through the first week on about $30! (There were just the two of us, and we didn't have to worry about feeding the masses.) The second week, we splurged and spent about $40. Still, we realized a savings of over $50 a week or $200 a month.

Another savings method is to shop with coupons. Shortly after getting married, we found a store that doubled the face-value of our coupons! We were saving anywhere from $5 to $20 in coupons every time we went shopping. Now, after applying the techniques in this book, our debt load is much more manageable, and we have guiltlessly returned to the restaurants and fast food shops on an occasional basis. But, we also find ourselves firing up the barbecue and eating at home at least five or six nights a week. That is the beauty of this system. When you are not overwhelmed by your debts and when you are not living from paycheck to paycheck, you do not have to feel guilty about pampering yourself a bit.

Where else can you save? What about the newspaper? If when you open it up, you go straight to the comics or your horoscope, then fold it back up and cancel your subscription today. You can catch up on the latest news on TV or the radio. The same thing goes for those magazines. If you use them just to decorate the coffee table, you don't need them. Besides, dusting is a snap if there's nothing to dust around.

Other expenses often found to be unnecessary are pay television channels or cable television altogether. Personally (my wife disagrees), I think I need the cable because we can't even pick up the local stations clearly without the cable hookup. But I *can* do without the pay channels, at least for a little while anyway. When we need a movie fix, we rent a video.

Sending all of your laundry to the dry cleaners may be another practice you'll want to reconsider. The maid who comes in once or twice a week is probably not all that necessary either. The purpose here is not to make your life more difficult, only more affordable. Keep telling yourself, it's only temporary. And if it is something you really think you need, or even something you really enjoy, keep it! Don't make this any harder than it has to be. Do without some things—don't do without others. And remember, these are only suggestions.

The membership at the local spa or health club could also go if you are not using it on a <u>very</u> regular basis. Once a month is not regular enough to justify the expense. You can always go jogging through the neighborhood for free.

"I'll lower my cholesterol if you lower your spending. Did I say that?"

What are you driving? Are you paying $250 a month or more on a car that you really don't need? Chances are you could sell your car, pay off the loan and have some money left over to apply toward other debts. If not, it might still pay you to give the car to someone who will just take over the payments. Besides, there is a car lot on every corner that has a nice car with air conditioning and radio for under $2000. Watch the classified adds. You'll be surprised at the deals that go through there. Then when you are debt free, pay cash for that dream car.

Where do you live? Could you do with less? Does it make sense to sell, use the equity, and start out fresh? Only you can determine what is or isn't right for you. You may want to refer back to Chapter Four for some other cost cutting measures when it comes to your home mortgage.

We have some friends who decided to move closer to the city. They were renting and commuting about 45-minutes to work at the time. The commute and rush hour traffic became unbearable, so they began looking closer in. They left a two bedroom, two bathroom apartment at $225 a month for a nicer condo downtown at over $400 a month. Of course, that is still a deal for most parts of the country, but considering what they were paying at first, a little steep. Because the condo provided racquetball courts, swimming pool, sauna, and recreational activities, they figured they would save enough in entertainment expenses to justify the increased rent.

To make a long story short, they only stayed in their condo for about six months. They moved back to where they were to begin with, deeper in debt, and had to pay all the utility hookup charges all over again. Plus the landlord had since increased rent on that property to $315. If they'd stayed with the original contract, their rent would have stayed at $225. If you can sacrifice a little today, you are almost guaranteed to be driving whatever you want, living in whatever you want and wherever you want, and doing everything you've ever dreamed of. Only you can decide, however, what you will sacrifice today to be where you want to be tomorrow.

A Warning

It will become very tempting when you begin working that extra job or when you eliminate the unnecessary expenses in life, to say, "Now that we have this extra income, we can afford that new sofa or that weekend in Las Vegas." DON'T DO IT!!! The reward for all of your efforts and sacrificing is getting out of debt ... not a new wardrobe. The new wardrobe can come after you are out of debt. Think about the money you could be saving, investing, or putting aside for that cruise to the Bahamas. Think about that evening out on the town you could have each week if you didn't have to spend your hard earned money paying off your creditors.

Avoid undue celebrations until you are debt free. That is not to say you should never treat yourself to a night out. If you don't pamper yourself a little, your path to debt free living will be miserable and the chance you will abandon it will be much greater. Reward yourself as you go, but make sure the reward is appropriate and reasonable.

The World of Insurance

Another area where you may be able to cut back is with your insurance coverage. Read over this section carefully. It may open your eyes. If you drive, you obviously understand the need to have car insurance, not to mention the legal obligation. If you rent or own your residence, you are most likely aware of the benefit of renter's insurance or home owner's insurance. But there are other types of insurance that few people understand, but that most have a need for: health and life insurance.

What follows is not meant to be the comprehensive and complete encyclopedia of life and health insurance. This section is meant, however, to alert you to the importance of the subject and give you the basics with which you can then go out and ask intelligent questions without getting suckered into buying something you do not need.

What type of insurance is best? Who should I buy it from? How much should I pay, and how much do I need? You could ask those questions to twenty different agents from twenty different insurance companies, and you would probably get twenty different answers. First, let's look at life insurance.

If there is only one piece of advice regarding life insurance that you remember and take to heart, it should be this: *Life insurance is not for you! It is for those you leave behind.* If you are single with no parents or surviving relatives dependent upon you, you do not need it. If you are in this category, skip to the section covering health and disability insurance. If you are not in this category, read on. Life insurance has several important purposes. Among them:

- It provides money to pay burial expenses and outstanding debts at the time of death.

- It protects your survivors against loss of income.

- It can serve as a form of savings for retirement.

The amount you pay for your premium is determined by several factors:

- The risk or likelihood that you will die. (Younger, healthier individuals pay less, older or ill individuals pay more.)

- The size of the benefit to be paid at death or retirement. (The larger the policy, the more it will cost you.)

- The administrative and sales fees charged by the company.

- The type of policy you decide to buy.

How Much Do I Need?

To determine how much life insurance to buy you will have to do a few calculations. In short, you will have to determine how much it will take for your spouse, children and other dependents to maintain their current standard of living in your absence. Keep in mind that you will need to include the cost of funeral and burial expenses, your family's living expenses, outstanding home mortgage and other debts, children's college expenses and your spouse's retirement.

Most financial planners estimate you will need about 75% of your current take-home pay after paying your outstanding debts. Keep in mind that the amount of life insurance you will need could be lessened by the amount your survivors would receive from pension or retirement plans, savings, social security, etc. The following worksheet is set up to help you determine just how much your family will need in your absence. There are additional worksheets in Appendix B.

Life Insurance Worksheet

I. Cash Needs
   A. Funeral and burial expenses $ 15,000 $ _____
   B. Probate and estate taxes   12,500   _____
     (Estimate 5% of gross estate.)
   C. Outstanding debts, including home mortgage.   102,000   _____
     (Use the total from the Current Balance column
     of your Debt Elimination Schedule on page 25.)
   D. Emergency fund   7,750   _____
     (Equal to three months of your total take home pay.)
   E. *College fund (Current cost of college for four   74,400   _____
     years multiplied by the number of children.)

   Total (lines A through E)   = $ 211,650   = _____

II. Annual Income Needs
   A. Annual income needed to maintain your family's   37,500   _____
     current standard of living.
     (Figure 75-80% of your current gross income.)
   B. Less annual Social Security benefits to be paid   -   18,875   - _____
     to your surviving dependents. (Call the Social
     Security Department at 800-772-1213 for an
     estimate of your annual S.S. benefit.)
   C. Less spouse's annual income   -   12,000   - _____
   D. Less any other annual income (Estimated   -   0   - _____
     investment/IRA distributions.)

   Total (Item IIA minus items IIB, IIC, & IID)   = $ 6,625   = _____

III. Retirement plan for spouse/family
   A. Amount from total at end of Section II.   6,625   _____
   B. Multiply amount from the line above by the   =   132,500   = _____
     number of years income will be needed.
     (Example assumes 20 years.)

IV. Available assets
   A. Assets currently available (Cash, stocks, etc.)   3,200   _____

V. Insurance Needed
   A. Cash needs from total in Section I. $ 211,650   _____
   B. Plus annual income/retirement needs from
     Section IIIB.   +   132,500   + _____
   C. Minus available assets from Section IV.   -   3,200   - _____

   Total insurance needed.   = $ 340,950   = _____
   (Item A plus item B, minus item C.)

NOTE:
  This worksheet is for illustrative purposes only. To determine your exact insurance needs you should consult with an estate planning attorney or financial planner.

* In the event of your death, insurance proceeds in this amount would be deposited as a lump sum into a savings/investment account until needed. It is assumed that interest earned during the interim should exceed the rate of inflation, thereby maintaining the same purchasing power.

Now that you have a better idea of how much insurance you should have, you will need to decide which type of insurance to buy. If you currently have insurance, you will want to pay particular attention to this section as you may discover that your current policy provides either too much, not enough, or the wrong type of coverage for your needs.

Term Insurance

Term insurance is the simplest form of life insurance, the most inexpensive and the one, perhaps, with the greatest benefit to the majority of the population. Term insurance pays benefits only at the time of death of the person insured. This type of insurance is most useful when a large amount of coverage is needed or if income is low. Term insurance is highly recommended for those who are students, for young married couples with few or no children, and for those who are heavily in debt. Term insurance is also ideal for those who will be financially independent because of a savings or pension plan at retirement.

Term insurance provides coverage for a certain period of time, usually in one to five-year increments, after which the premium typically goes up.

Term insurance comes in two basic varieties: renewable and non-renewable. With renewable term you qualify for renewal at the end of the policy term, without a medical examination. Non-renewable, on the other hand, despite the name, is renewable, but only after requalifying at the end of the policy. Requalifying usually consists of taking a physical exam or at the least, filling out a health questionnaire. Non-renewable term insurance will be slightly less expensive but you should keep in mind that there are

drawbacks. Suppose you become terminally ill during the policy. It is likely you will not qualify for renewal or find any other insurer willing to write a policy on you if this is the case. With renewable term, the insurer would have no choice. You requalify automatically regardless of your health.

Renewable policies can be broken out further into two more subcategories: decreasing face-value and fixed face-value policies. With a decreasing face-value policy, the premium will remain the same over the years but the amount of insurance will decrease as you get older. With a fixed face-value policy you will pay a higher premium as you grow older but the amount of insurance will remain the same.

For term insurance, you can expect to pay only a few dollars per year for each $1,000 of insurance, depending, of course, on your age, health, sex and lifestyle. For example, a 35-year-old non-smoking man, might pay $200 a year for a $100,000 policy. This would break out to about $16 per month.

Convertible term policies are also available that can be converted to whole life policies without a medical examination.

Whole Life Insurance

Whole life insurance provides protection over your entire life span without an increase in premiums as you grow older. Policies that provide coverage throughout your life span are called permanent life insurance. This is in comparison to term insurance, which covers you for the period, or term, of the policy. For practical purposes, whole life insurance is nothing more than term life insurance with a savings plan added to it.

The way it works is quite simple. You pay your premium to the insurance company. The company takes enough out of your premium to pay for the insurance and then invests the remainder of the premium on your behalf. Most whole life policies will allow you to borrow against your policy as well. The interest you earn is also tax-deferred until you withdraw it. The cash value of your policy, (the amount your beneficiary gets if you die) always remains the same.

The disadvantages to whole life insurance policies are that the premiums are higher than term insurance. There are also commissions and management fees attached because of the investment side of the policy. Another disadvantage is that most insurance companies' investment portfolios are weighted with bonds and mortgages, both instruments that rise and fall with interest rates.

Many financial advisors argue that you would do better to pay the lower premiums and get term insurance and invest the difference in what you would pay for whole life elsewhere. Insurance sales people will argue, however, that the majority of the population will not invest the difference and this "forced savings" is the only way to go.

Universal Life Insurance

There are a variety of insurance hybrids that combine some of the characteristics of term and whole life insurance with other investment options. Universal life insurance combines a term insurance policy with an interest-earning savings account that is geared to current market rates. This investment portion is usually locked into money-market funds. And, unlike whole life insurance, the cash value or death benefit can grow as the interest you earn

on your investments grows. Another plus to Universal life policies is that the insurer will provide you with an annual report showing you exactly where you stand and what your policy is costing you and earning you. Universal life policies will usually allow the policy holder to skip premium payments after the policy has built up a certain cash value. The insurer will then deduct your premiums from the "equity" built up in the policy.

Variable Life Insurance

Variable life insurance is similar to whole life and universal life in that a portion of your premium goes to cover the basic insurance and the balance of your premium is then invested. The difference with variable life is that most of the investment decisions are left up to you. The carrier will often let you change investment vehicles during the year so long as the vehicle you choose is included in the carrier's investment portfolio.

There are also a number of other hybrid insurance policies that combine the benefits of term, whole, universal or variable life. Again, if your main purpose is providing income protection for survivors in case of death, term insurance is most likely the way to go. It gives the greatest amount of coverage and protection at the lowest cost. For persons, however, who would not be able to meet their savings goals without a carefully administered system, one of these other types of insurance may be the answer.

Select your insurance plan with care. But keep in mind, it is often less expensive and will actually make more money for you in the long run to buy separate components of the plans available and to invest the difference elsewhere.

Remember also that the greater the coverage and the more enticing the policy, the more it will cost you. Another factor to keep in mind with regard to many insurance policies is that the insurance companies will also set a target premium that you will have to pay in order keep your policy in full force. If you cannot afford their current target premiums, you will probably not be able to keep the policy long enough for it to do you any good.

Countless individuals have been persuaded to buy expensive insurance policies with attractive savings plans only to find out down the road that they can't afford the premiums. They stop making their payments, lose the policy and lose a lot of money in the meantime.

A word to those just starting out:

If you are still not fully employed in the career you are embarking on, if you are a student still struggling through school, or if you are heavily in debt, it simply does not make sense to be paying the high premiums associated with most life insurance policies. The excuses and reasons to pay the higher rates are many:

- Just look at what I am worth with this policy.

- I'm getting a 15% return on my money.

- My family will never have to worry about getting by if I die.

- My agent got me a really good deal.

- I can't cancel my policy, I'll lose everything I've paid in.

- My choice of career probably won't

provide me with adequate insurance coverage.

- The difference between buying now and buying in a couple of years could cost me millions of dollars by the time I turn 65.

But despite these reasons, if you are in one of the situations mentioned earlier—a student, newly married, or deeply in debt—you most likely cannot afford the premiums you are paying for anything other than term insurance.

If you are middle-aged or better (you will have to determine what "middle-aged" means) and have been paying for your policy for a number of years, you may need to keep what you have and figure out a way to make the payments. Also, if you only have a few years before the policy starts paying its own premiums, you may want to keep the policy as well.

But if you are paying high premiums and you can't meet all of your monthly obligations, chances are you are going to lose the policy anyway. Why not cancel it now before you lose even more!

Students and young married couples often get suckered into buying policies they don't need or can't afford. The fact is insurance salesmen look through the wedding announcements of every newspaper in town to find their next sale.

Other things to consider: If you are embarking on a career where you will most likely be with a large company or firm, it will probably provide you with life insurance at reduced or very reasonable rates. In the meantime, all you need is term insurance in case you die. Remember, that is the real purpose behind insurance ... coverage for your loved ones if you pass away.

The 10% or 12% returns of some life insurance policies are not any better than 3¼% earned in a bank savings account, if you are paying 22% interest on your debts. Concentrate on getting out of debt first: maintain a term policy in the event of the unexpected, and then later, once you are debt free, you can begin concentrating on your savings.

There are also IRAs, bonds, money-market funds, etc., that you can invest in at the appropriate time. On average, they will also provide you with higher rates of return than you will get from your fancy insurance policies. And best of all, if you have to skip a payment or contribution on these savings instruments, you don't lose your money, which is not always the case with insurance policies.

Bottom line ... if you die, a $100,000 insurance policy is worth exactly $100,000 whether you pay $16 a month for term or $100 a month for universal. Be realistic and only buy what you need. Don't be bullied or intimidated into buying something you don't need. It doesn't matter if the agent is a friend, family member, or otherwise—you must guard your hard earned money.

Health Insurance

If you work for a large company, you are likely already covered. Just be sure you keep abreast of changes in the policy requirements and follow the "rules" to the letter. There is nothing worse than having coverage that won't pay up because you failed to make a phone call first or because you failed to file the proper form.

If you work for a smaller company that doesn't cover your health insurance or if you are self-employed, there are several Health Maintenance Organizations (HMOs)

and Blue Cross agencies at your disposal. Get your insurance before you need it. Once you are sick, it will cost you much more.

If you currently do not have health insurance, put down this book, go to the phone book and start calling around for quotes. Some of the best buys can be found through group policies and are offered to members of various clubs, trade groups, credit unions, etc.

You may find that you can gain access to very reasonable coverage by simply joining your local credit union. Many policies will even let you pay and renew on a month-to-month basis.

Don't overlook the big names like Blue Cross/Blue Shield. You can often find coverage from these organization for less than the so-called "no-name" companies.

Things to avoid are insurances that only cover one type of disease or "accidents only." Make sure you are covered for everything: disease, accidents, natural disasters, etc.

You are probably well advised to avoid mail order policies or health insurance sold on late-night television. If you do decide to go this route, be sure to check first with your local Better Business Bureau or Consumer Protection Agency.

Disability Insurance

So you've got your insurance. Great! Now, if you die, you are covered. If you get sick, you are covered. But what if you get hit by a falling satellite (I watch too much T.V.) and don't die, but become permanently disabled. There are literally thousands of individuals who find themselves bed-ridden or in a wheelchair through an accident of some sort, with no way to earn a living and provide for their family. In this situation savings typically last only a month or two, and the burden then falls on the family.

Disability insurance can be your saving grace from this type of situation. Disability insurance begins paying you if you become sick or injured and cannot work. The cost of the insurance and length of the coverage will vary from policy to policy. Many policies will cover you for life. Others, like term insurance, are renewable from year to year. Again, don't wait until it's too late to go shopping for this type of coverage.

Where There's a Will, There's a Way

Nobody should be preoccupied with death. But by the same token, nobody should ignore the realities. It is a fact; we will all, one day, die. So what about preparing a will? It's only necessary for rich folks, for older people, or for those with a large number of assets, right? Wrong!

If you have any assets at all or any surviving family members, a will is one of the most important documents you will ever sign. If you do not have a will, the state in which you reside will write it for you. In other words, the state decides for you who gets your property and who becomes the legal guardian of your children.

What exactly is a will? A will is a formal document drawn up and signed by you that specifies, point by point, how you want your assets distributed, who will be the guardian of your minor children and often explains your desired funeral arrangements. Your will should also name

an executor, or the person who will handle the details of your estate after your death. Your executor does not have to be a lawyer—just a responsible adult. Your spouse or any of your grown children would usually be acceptable.

As mentioned, earlier, all states already have some laws on their books dictating all of these things for you, should you not have a properly drawn, signed and witnessed will.

For example, your assets might go half to your children and half to your surviving spouse. If your spouse remarries, your assets could become the property of his or her new spouse with no guarantee that any of your assets will ever go to your children. The state will also decide for you, how much, if any, of your estate will go to your parents and siblings.

So what do you need to do? In short, have a will prepared. It does not have to be elaborate or an unreasonably uncomfortable process. Attorneys specializing in wills and trusts can be found in the yellow pages of your local phone directory. Simple wills can start as low as $50 to $75. A more elaborate will might cost upwards of $500.

Although it is not recommended, you can even write your will yourself. Your local library will have several books available to help you. The problem, though, with writing your own will, is that the courts are then left to interpret it.

For example, when you left everything to Uncle John and his children, did that mean to Uncle John's estate if he dies? Did it mean divided between Uncle John and his eight children equally? What if Uncle John remarries and his new wife brings children into the marriage? Do they get part of your estate?

Perhaps you are thinking, "If I die, the state in which I reside dictates that my entire estate and the custody of my children will be turned over to my spouse." This may be the case. But what if you are both killed at the same time in an automobile accident. Who then will be granted custody of your children? Will it be your parents, your brother, or your sister? Will it be the State Social Services Department? Who will be the executor of your estate? Are you willing to risk letting the state decide?

The process of determining your desires as outlined in your will is called probate. The word "probate" comes from a latin word meaning "to prove." And true to its meaning, all wills must first be presented to a probate court for the court to determine the validity of the will. If the will was not properly prepared or witnessed, even if you personally drew it up yourself, the probate judge can decide to ignore the will's instructions.

If the will is determined to be valid, the executor will be notified or one appointed if there is not one named in the will. The executor will then notify the affected parties, such as beneficiaries, creditors, etc. From there all taxes, creditors and other fees will have to be satisfied. Finally, beneficiaries will receive their distribution from your estate and the estate will be closed. This probate process can take anywhere from six months to over two years.

All wills are subject to this probate process regardless of whether they were drawn up by an attorney or by you. The difference is that the professionally prepared wills normally pass through probate quickly and with relative ease. Those drawn up by individuals are the ones that typically end up in lengthy court battles.

The only exception to wills passing through probate are when, if you die, <u>all</u> of your property and assets are considered non-probate. Non-probate would be anything jointly owned and recognized in the state you reside as passing to the co-owner. An example would be a house jointly titled with rights of survivorship included in the title. Don't speculate what the laws of your state are. Find out and then hire a competent attorney to help you through the process of drawing up your will.

An alternative to a will is a living trust. Like a will, a living trust is established while you are alive (thus the "living") but is not subject to probate after you die. Simple living trusts can usually be established by an estate planning attorney for around $500. There are two types of living trusts: revocable and irrevocable. Revocable trusts can be altered or annulled by you at a later date. An irrevocable trust does not have that option.

There are three key players to a living trust. And often, one person can perform all three of these functions. The trust needs to have a grantor, the person who sets up the trust; a trustee who will manage the assets after they have been placed in the trust; and finally, a beneficiary or beneficiaries who receive the distributions from the trust. Many states will even let you handle all three of these responsibilities for your own trust. You, of course, will need to name a trustee to handle your estate once you die or if you become unable to manage the estate in your old age.

Anyone who has been through the process of dividing up an estate or going through probate can tell you how important it is to plan ahead. Nobody wants to participate in a lengthy court battle. Death should not be a time to divide families that would normally draw together after the loss of a loved one. If you have not yet made arrangements for your estate, your spouse, or your children after your death—go to the library, study it out, and then hire a competent attorney to help you through the process. The $50 you spend for a legally recognized will or trust is a bargain when you consider the consequences of not having one!

Chapter Six

Dealing with Credit Bureaus
and Credit Reports

*Few people recognize opportunity because
it comes disguised as hard work.*
- Cary Grant

The age in which we live is an age of credit. That should come as no great revelation or surprise to you. Credit has become not only the accepted way of life, but all too often the necessary way of life. No longer can you rely on your charismatic personality, your good name, or even your parent's good name to get you by. In today's world, more times than not, you are recognized only as a Social Security number or as a name attached to a credit report. If you don't yet have credit or if you have poor credit, you are probably finding yourself at a serious disadvantage.

If, on the other hand, your credit and credit reports are handled correctly, they can be the very vehicles that will take you to your desired destinations in life. This chapter will teach you how to turn your credit report into the financial passport of your future. In the next few pages you will learn what credit bureaus are, what they do and don't do, and how to locate them. You will also learn how to find out what information they have about you in their files, and finally how to repair negative marks that may show up in your record.

Beware of Credit Repair Fraud!

The advertisements can be found in virtually every classified section of every newspaper in the country. "Credit Problems? No Problem!" "Erase Bad Credit! 100% Guaranteed." "Remove bankruptcy and liens from your credit file." "VISA/MasterCard without a credit check." My advice to you is to beware of such come-ons!

People or businesses making claims such as these most likely will take your money and vanish. And even if they do remain in business, you can almost be assured that there will be strings attached and that their services will cost you more money than you can afford to lose. In fact, federal officials estimate that credit-repair scams are costing consumers upwards of $100 million a year. Don't be fooled. Anything these credit repair agencies claim they can do for you, you can do for yourself.

If you have a bad credit history, no one can unconditionally guarantee to clean it up for you and get you new credit. Although errors can be corrected, a poor credit history cannot be erased overnight.

But don't give up hope, because you *can* take steps to resolve your credit woes. Solving them, however, will take time, patience, and some understanding of the law.

Who Are They and What Are They Saying About You?

"They" ... are the credit reporting agencies or credit bureaus. There are three major credit reporting networks with local offices in thousands of cities nationwide. They are: TRW, Trans Union, and Equifax. Although any one of the three major bureaus or agencies may be stronger than another in a given section of the country, all provide services nationwide. In fact, these three credit reporting agencies maintain and keep track of credit information on over 170 million people, making them second only to the Social Security Department in the amount of information they keep on file. They process in excess of 24 billion pieces of information a year in their systems and

"Hello credit bureau, I need to check my file."

generate 1.5 million credit reports a day, or, 450 million reports each year.

Exactly what do these credit reporting agencies do? Well, they gather information on credit users and sell that information, in the form of credit reports, to credit grantors such as banks, finance companies, and retailers. Credit bureaus keep records of consumers' debts and how regularly these debts are repaid. Anything and everything that is paid over time can, and most likely will, show up on these reports: credit cards, installment loans, other credit accounts, and mortgages, just to name a few.

The reports the agencies generate and send out inform the requester whether payments are up-to-date or overdue, or if any action has ever been taken to collect overdue bills. The information is usually updated monthly.

They also provide information on where you live and work, and what your salary is, and they may note a number of items of public record, such as bankruptcies or judgments against you.

This information is then used by potential lenders to determine whether you will be a good credit risk. It can also be used by potential employers trying to find out more about your character, reliability, and stability.

So where do these credit bureaus get all this information? They get it from the people you regularly do business with. Banks, retail stores, finance companies, credit unions and virtually anyone else involved in the selling or financing of goods or services will be registered with one of the major credit bureaus and will regularly provide the bureau with information on how you handle your account. Many credit bureaus will then

share that information with other credit bureaus via a central computer system.

Think about it. If every time you filled out an application for credit the credit manager had to call all over town to see if you pay your bills on time, this would become quite time consuming and expensive. Besides, many of the people you deal with might not want to give out that kind of information to the credit manager. So what does the credit manager do? He subscribes as a member to one of the major credit reporting agencies. He then can simply call or FAX the bureau, give them his authorization/membership number and request an updated credit report on you.

How Time Affects Your Credit Report

Credit reporting agencies can, by law, report most negative information for up to seven years. The seven-year period runs from the date of the last regularly scheduled payment that was made before the account became delinquent, unless the creditor took action on the account, such as charging it off or obtaining a judgment for the amount due. If action was taken, the seven years would begin on the date of the action.

For example, if you were delinquent on your new sofa payments and the furniture store turned the account over to a collection agency, the credit bureau could keep this on your file for seven years from the date the collection agency was called in.

There are exceptions to the seven-year time period. Bankruptcies, for example, may be reported for up to ten years. It

"Your personal credit file......Enjoy."

should also be noted that in at least three circumstances, credit information can be reported indefinitely.

1. If you apply for $50,000 or more in credit;

2. If you apply for a life insurance policy with a face value of $50,000 or more;

3. If you apply for a job paying $20,000 or more (and the employer requests a credit report in connection with the job application).

Although the seven-year allowance does exist, under most circumstances credit reporting agencies will have their own rules and regulations, and the reporting periods will be much shorter.

Most agencies will only report inquiries

into your account for about six months to two years. This information will become important to you as you begin to establish, clean-up or increase your credit.

Obtaining a Copy of Your Credit Report

Many consumers have no idea what their credit reports say about them. Others fear their reports will be entirely negative, so they shy away from ever looking at them. For these people, ignorance and comfort are apparently the same thing. And there is still another group of people who naively believe their credit reports are spotless because they keep getting credit card offers in the mail. All too often, reality sets in when they go to purchase that new car or home and find long forgotten skeletons that should have been cleaned from their file years ago. No longer do you need to fall into any of these categories.

In order for you to successfully follow this section of the course, it will be necessary for you to get a copy of your credit report. If for no other reason, you need to have the peace of mind that comes with knowing where your credit history stands. You will also need some of the information on your report as your financial future begins to unfold. Most financial advisors recommend that consumers review their credit files regularly, every two to four years. So this will hopefully be the beginning of a good habit on your part.

Despite what you may hear from most "credit repair" companies, there are no secret formulas needed to contact or deal with credit bureaus. The process is quite simple and is really no more complicated than tracking down any other business in town. The best way to find them will probably be to contact your creditors and ask them which credit bureaus they subscribe to. Other than that, you can "let your fingers do the walking." Consult your local phone directory. Look under headings such as "Credit," "Credit Bureaus," or "Credit Reporting Agencies." Phone numbers and addresses should help you determine which agencies are closest to you.

In addition to contacting the local bureaus in your area, you should also contact each of the three major credit reporting agencies and ask them for any information they have on you in their files. (The addresses and phone numbers of the three major reporting agencies are included at the end of Chapter Seven.) When contacting them, be sure to include all the necessary identifying information they will need to honor your request. Identifying information includes your full name, maiden name (if applicable), your spouse's name if a making a joint request, Social Security number, your spouses Social Security number if joint, current address, former addresses for the past five years, birth dates for you and spouse if a joint request, and verification of your name and address. Verification can be a photocopy of your driver's license or a utility bill with your current name and address on it. Also, be sure to sign your request. If it appears as though this is a tedious process to request information, you are right. And you should be pleased. This process was put into place to protect you and ensure that information on you is not made available to parties that should not receive it.

Although many back-alley "credit-repair" companies will tell you there are certain forms that "you must use" or forms that "get results" when dealing with the credit bureaus, this simply is not true. You can format or word your requests however you please. The bureaus are bound by federal law to respond to your request. There are sample letters for dealing with credit bureaus included in Appendix C. You do not need to copy these letters word for word. Simply write to the bureau and make your request. It is as simple as that.

You should not be charged when a credit bureau checks to see if it has you on file. Most bureaus will, however, charge a fee (around $15) to actually give you a copy of your credit report.

Also, credit bureaus and credit reporting agencies normally will not give out information over the phone. Instead, they will require you to make your request in writing or to make an appointment and come, in person, to their office. If you make a personal visit, be sure to take with you two forms of picture identification, or one picture I.D. and a birth certificate. When you arrive at their office a representative will review your file with you. Remember they are not a government-run organization, nor are they a credit repair company. They are in business solely to provide information to credit grantors in return for a profit. They will show you your file only because federal law forces them to do so.

All too often, consumers go in thinking the bureau is a branch of the government and that they not only have to give them their file, but help them develop a plan to clean it up as well. This is not the case. Thus, it is to your benefit to be extremely patient and pleasant with the bureau representatives. If you are, they probably will be courteous and helpful in return.

New laws are also constantly being passed governing credit bureaus and making it easier for consumers to get information about them in the bureau files. Each of the reporting agencies is also constantly trying to find new ways to improve their relationships with consumers.

Many of the things they are doing are a result of in-house reviews and suggestions but some of the recent changes have stemmed from a number of lawsuits and complaints filed with the Federal Trade Commission. In fact, credit bureaus have become the largest category of consumer complaints at the FTC.

Among the complaints registered most frequently: not being able to find a phone number, address or customer service department at the bureaus to listen to complaints; slow response time when complaints are registered; and lax procedures to ensure accuracy of reports.

In 1992, all three of the major credit reporting agencies initiated new policies and procedures to help curtail the number of consumer complaints. TRW for example is now offering consumers one free copy of their credit report each year. All three of the bureaus have revamped their credit reporting formats making them more "user friendly" or easier to read and interpret.

All three have also set up consumer assistance centers and phone numbers to handle questions, concerns and requests.

On that note, don't be shy or hesitant about calling or sitting down with one of the credit bureau representatives. You have the right to know what is in your credit report. The bureaus will not try to sell you anything, nor will they lecture you on the contents of your file. What they will do is show you your file. Most will also answer questions you have concerning it.

If you have been denied credit within the past 60 days, they are required by law to provide you a copy of your credit report free of charge. (Until recently the grace period for a free copy of your report was 30-days).

If denied credit, a consumer also now has the right to receive a free copy of the report from each of the three major credit reporting agencies. The process to follow if you have been denied credit is described later in this chapter.

If you have not been denied credit in the past 60 days, they may ask why you want to see your file. Just be honest. Tell them you are in the process of taking care of some of your debts and that you need to know what is on file to better organize your plan of action.

Some credit reporting agencies have membership services that can be of tremendous help when it comes to obtaining copies of your credit report and understanding them. There are, of course, annual membership fees for this service, usually around $40 per year. For some, the fee will be money well spent; for others, a wasted $40. The pros and cons of these service are outlined below.

Pros:

As a subscriber to such a service you may become entitled to:

1. Copies of your credit report whenever you wish at no additional charge.

2. Notification whenever anyone requests or receives a copy of your credit report.

3. Step-by-step instructions to help you understand everything in your credit report.

4. All the forms necessary to update or dispute items in your credit report.

5. All services may be provided for your spouse at no additional charge.

Cons:

1. The law already grants you the right to see your file as often as you like. And if you only need a copy of your credit file an average of once a year, you can get this by paying the bureau their standard fee, usually around $15, which is a savings of $25 if you don't join the club!

2. You will typically already know when someone is going to check your file because you will have filled out an application for credit, housing, employment, etc., thus triggering the credit inquiry.

Although you don't need to subscribe to one of these services, if you do, the difficulty of dealing with credit bureaus will almost be immediately eliminated, or at least reduced. The largest agency with this service is TRW. The address for TRW Credentials Service is included at the end of Chapter Seven.

Understanding Your Report

Once you have located the agency or agencies with your name on file, there are a couple of things you need to understand. One is that, contrary to popular belief, credit bureaus do not track all aspects of your personal life, nor do they evaluate credit applications. Credit bureaus are simply organizations that collect and transmit four principal types of information.

1. Identification and employment data: Your name, birth date, address, Social Security number, spouse's name, and employer are routinely noted. The bureau also may provide other information, such as your employment history, home ownership, income, and previous address (if a creditor requests it).

2. Payment history: Your account records with different creditors are listed, showing how much credit

has been extended to you and how you have repaid it. Related events, such as referrals of overdue accounts to collection agencies may also be noted.

3. Inquiries: Credit bureaus are required to maintain a record of all creditors who have requested a copy of your file in the recent past. They normally include such inquiries in your credit file for at least six months and often longer.

4. Public record information: Events that are a matter of public record and are related to your credit-worthiness, such as bankruptcies, foreclosures, or tax liens, may also appear in your report.

Once you have a copy of your credit report, you will find that most of the information is self-explanatory. And although each bureau may use a different format, the information provided is fundamentally the same. The sample credit report, included on pages 75 and 76, is the one used by Equifax, one of the "big-three" credit reporting agencies.

The top half of the report provides background information such as your name, spouse's name, address, and Social Security number. The rest of the report is simply a listing of information about accounts and payment histories. You will want to pay special attention to the "Balance" and "Past Due" sections. The "Balance" is the amount still owed, the "Past Due" column will detail how many days or months past due a bill is. Some reports may include a column called the "Status" or "Account Profile," which will give a rating assigned by the creditor. The most common ratings will be positive, negative or non-rated. The Status column

may also indicate if the account is being paid as agreed or if it is past due.

The three types of credit referred to on the report will normally be listed as an **open 30-day** agreement, a **revolving** credit account, or installment credit. These may also be listed with identifying letters such as **O, R,** or **I.**

- In an **open 30-day** agreement, a consumer promises to repay the full balance owed each month. Travel-and-entertainment charge cards (such as American Express) and charge accounts with local businesses often require full repayment each month.

- In a **revolving** credit agreement, a consumer has the option of paying the balance due, in full, each month or of making a minimum payment based on the amount of the balance outstanding. Department stores, gas and oil companies, and banks typically issue credit cards based on a revolving credit plan.

- In an **installment** credit agreement, a consumer signs a contract to repay a fixed amount of credit in equal payments over a specified period of time. Automobiles, furniture, and major appliances are often purchased on an installment basis. Personal loans are usually paid in installments as well.

The bottom of the report lists previous addresses, employment history, accounts gone to collection, inquiries and if any judgments have been filed against the consumer. This is also where the consumer is allowed to include his side of the story if he feels information in his report is inaccurate or should not be

EQUIFAX
The Information Source

CREDIT INFORMATION
SERVICES

Sample Credit Report

The Name and Address of the Equifax office you should contact if you have any questions or disagreement with your credit report.

EQUIFAX SAMPLE REPORT OFFICE
BUSINESS ADDRESS
CITY, STATE 00000
PHONE NUMBER

I.D. Section

Your name, current address and other identifying information reported by your creditors.

Please address all future correspondence to the address shown on right. ➧

JOHN DOE
123 HOME ADDRESS
CITY, STATE 00000

DATE 06/04/91
SOCIAL SECURITY NUMBER 123-45-6789
DATE OF BIRTH 12/01/60
SPOUSE JANE

Credit History Section

List of open and paid accounts indicating any late payments reported by your creditors.

CREDIT HISTORY

The first item identifies the business that is reporting the information.

This is your account number with the company reporting.

Number of months account payment history has been reported.

This is the month and year you opened the account with the credit grantor.

See explanation below.

This is the date of last activity on the account and may be the date of last payment or the date of last charge.

The highest amount charged or the credit limit.

Represents number of installments (M=Months) or monthly payment.

The amount owed on the account at the time it was reported.

This figure indicates any amount past due at the time the information was reported.

Date of last account update.

(See explanation below)

Company Name	Account Number	Whose Acct.	Date Opened	Months Reviewed	Date Of Last Activity	High Credit	Terms	All Items as of Date Reported			Date Reported
								Balance	Past Due	Status	
SEARS	11251514	I	05/86	66	10/91	3500		0		R1	12/91
C&S	2953900000100473	I	11/86	48	11/90	9388	48M	0		I1	11/90
AMEX	355411251511	I	06/87	24	10/91	500		0		O1	12/91
FNB	54229778	I	05/85	48	10/91	5000	340	3000	680	R3	12/91

> > > PRIOR PAYING HISTORY — 30(03) 60(04) 90+(01) 08/90-R2, 02/89-R3, 10/88-R4 < < <

Number of times account was either 30/60/90 days past due.

Date two most recent delinquencies occurred plus date of most severe delinquency.

Collection Accounts

Accounts which your creditors turned over to a collection agency.

COLLECTION ACCOUNTS

> > > COLLECTION REPORTED 06/90, ASSIGNED TO PRO COLL 09/89, CLIENT-ABC HOSP
AMOUNT-$978, UNPAID 06/90, BALANCE-$978 06/90
DATE OF LAST ACTIVITY 09/89, INDIVIDUAL, ACCOUNT NUMBER 787652JC

Courthouse Records

Public Record items obtained from local, state and federal courts which reflect your history of meeting financial obligations.

COURTHOUSE RECORDS

> > > LIEN FILED 03/88, FULTON CTY, CASE NUMBER-32114, AMOUNT-$26667, CLASS-CITY/COUNTY
RELEASED 07/88, VERIFIED 09/90

> > > BANKRUPTCY FILED 12/89, FULTON CTY, CASE NUMBER-673HC12, LIABILITIES-$15787, PERSONAL
INDIVIDUAL, DISCHARGED, ASSETS-$780

> > > JUDGMENT FILED 07/87, FULTON CTY, CASE NUMBER-898872, DEFENDANT-JOHN DOE
AMOUNT-$8984, PLAINTIFF-ABC REAL ESTATE, SATISFIED 03/89, VERIFIED 05/90

Additional Information

Primarily consists of former addresses and employments reported by your creditors.

ADDITIONAL INFORMATION

> > >FORMER ADDRESS 456 JUPITER, RD, ATLANTA, GA 30245

> > >FORMER ADDRESS P. O. BOX 2138, SAVANNAH, GA 31406

> > >CURRENT EMPLOYMENT ENGINEER, SPACE PATROL

Inquiry Section

List of businesses that have received your credit report in the last 24 months.

INQUIRY SECTION

·········· COMPANIES THAT REQUESTED YOUR CREDIT HISTORY ··········

06/04/91 EQUIFAX	06/03/90 GECC	08/30/89 MACYS
05/03/91 VISA	04/01/90 FIRST NATL	07/03/89 RICHS
02/13/91 SEARS	03/05/90 PRM VISA	06/20/91 C&S
01/23/91 JC PENNEY	01/03/90 SPEIGEL	06/03/91 FAMILY FIN

INQUIRIES NOT REPORTED TO CUSTOMERS

A PRM inquiry means that only your name and address were given to a credit grantor so they could offer you an application for credit.

An A/M or AR inquiry indicates a periodic review of your credit history by one of your creditors.

An Equifax inquiry indicates our activity in response to your request for a copy of your credit report.

PRM, AM, AR and Equifax inquiries do not show on credit reports that businesses receive, only on reports provided to you.

Whose Account

Indicates who is responsible for the account and the type of participation you have with the account.

- J = Joint
- I = Individual
- U = Undesignated
- A = Authorized user
- T = Terminated
- M = Maker
- C = Co-Maker/Co-Signer
- B = On behalf of another person
- S = Shared

Status

Type Of Account
- O = Open (entire balance due each month)
- R = Revolving (payment amount variable)
- I = Installment (fixed number of payments)

Timeliness Of Payment
- 0 = Approved not used
- 1 = Paid as agreed
- 2 = 30 days past due
- 3 = 60 days past due
- 4 = 90 days past due
- 5 = 120 days past due
- 7 = Making regular payments under wage earner plan or similar arrangement
- 8 = Repossesion
- 9 = Seriously delinquent/bad debt (paid or unpaid)

Length Of Time Information Remains In Your File

Credit and collection accounts — 7 years from date of last activity with original creditor.

Courthouse records— 7 years from date filed except Bankruptcy chapters 7 and 11 which remain for 10 years from date filed.

Note: New York State only. Satisified judgments 5 years from the date filed. Paid collections 5 years from date of last activity with original creditor.

included. The process of disputing items on your report is explained later in this chapter.

Other sections of the report that may need a brief explanation are:

- **Whose Account:**
  "J" indicates joint account with spouse contractually liable;

  "I" indicates account is sole responsibility of this individual.

  "A" indicates the consumer is an authorized user of this account;

  "T" indicates the account has been terminated.

- **Prior Paying History:**
  This area will tell potential creditors how many times an account was either 30, 60, or 90 days past due as well as the date the two most

recent delinquencies and the most severe delinquency occurred.

Know Your Rights And Use Them To Your Advantage

As was mentioned at the beginning of this chapter, there are no magical formulas or guaranteed ways to change the information in your credit report. That does not mean, however, that you are stuck if your file contains erroneous or inaccurate information. In fact, federal law requires that credit bureaus reinvestigate any items you dispute in a "reasonable amount of time" and that they remove or update the inaccurate information without charge to you.

The law that gives you these rights is known as the *Fair Credit Reporting Act* and was passed by the United States Congress on April 25, 1971. The sole purpose of this act is to protect consumers against the circulation of inaccurate or obsolete information and to ensure that consumer reporting agencies adopt fair and equitable procedures for obtaining, maintaining, and giving out information about consumers. Under this law there are certain rights which you have, and those rights cannot be denied. For instance, you have the right:

1. To be told the name and address of the credit reporting agency responsible for preparing a report that was used to deny you credit, insurance, or employment, or to increase the cost of credit or insurance.

2. To be told by a credit reporting agency the nature, substance, and sources of the information collected about you.

3. To take anyone of your choice with you when you visit the credit reporting agency to check your file.

4. To obtain, free of charge, all information to which you are entitled if the request is made within 30 days after receiving notification for denial of credit, insurance, or employment based on information contained in a credit report. (All three of the major credit reporting agencies now grant free reports within 60-days of denial). Otherwise, the reporting agency is permitted to charge a reasonable fee for giving you the information.

5. To be told who has received your credit report within the preceding six months, or within the preceding two years if the report was furnished for employment purposes.

6. To have incomplete or incorrect information reinvestigated unless the credit reporting agency has reasonable grounds to believe that the dispute is frivolous or irrelevant. If the information is investigated and found to be inaccurate, or if the information cannot be verified, you have the right to have such information removed from your file.

7. To have the reporting agency notify those you name (at no cost to you), who have previously received the incorrect or incomplete information, that this information has been deleted from your file.

8. When a dispute between you and the reporting agency about information in your file cannot be resolved, to have your version of such dispute placed in the file and included in future credit reports.

9. To request that the reporting agency send your version of the dispute to certain businesses without charge, if requested within 30 days of the adverse action.

10. To have a credit report withheld from anyone who under the law does not have a legitimate business need for the information.

11. To sue a reporting agency for damages if the agency willfully or negligently violates the law; and, if you are successful, to collect attorney's fees and court costs.

12. Not to have adverse information reported after seven years. One major exception is bankruptcy, which may be reported for 10 years.

13. To request from the business that ordered an investigative credit report more information about the nature and scope of the investigation.

14. To discover the nature and substance (but not the sources) of the information that was collected for an investigative credit report.

Now that you know what the *Fair Credit Reporting Act* does for you, you should also be aware that there are some things it does not do. For example, it does not:

1. Require the credit reporting agency to provide you with a copy of your file, although some agencies will voluntarily give you a copy.

2. Compel anyone to do business with an individual consumer.

3. Apply when you request commercial (as distinguished from consumer) credit or business insurance.

4. Authorize any federal agency to intervene on behalf of an individual consumer.

5. Require a credit reporting agency to add new accounts to your file; however, some agencies may do so for a fee.

Challenging The Powers That Be

Items six through nine detail your rights under the law when it comes to disputing negative or inaccurate information found on your report. These are the items credit-repair companies normally tell their clients they need help with. Again, this couldn't be further from the truth.

The process involved with challenging information in your credit report is very straightforward and can be completed with little, if any, assistance.

If you challenge information in your report, the credit bureau must reinvestigate it within a "reasonable period of time," unless it believes the dispute is "frivolous or irrelevant." To check on the accuracy of a disputed item, the credit bureau will ask the creditor in question what its records show. If the disputed item is a part of the public record, that information will be verified. If a disputed item cannot be confirmed, the credit bureau must delete it.

If an item contains erroneous information, the credit bureau must correct the error. If the item is incomplete, the bureau must complete it. For example, if your file lists accounts that belong to another person, the credit bureau would have to delete them. If it shows that you were, at one time, late in making payments but fails to show that you are no longer delinquent, the credit bureau would have to add information to show that your payments are now current.

Also, at your request, the credit bureau must send a notice of the correction to any creditor who has checked your file in the past six months.

If the reinvestigation does not resolve your dispute, the *Fair Credit Reporting Act* permits you to file a statement of up to 100 words with the credit bureau explaining your side of the situation.

Employees of the credit bureau are available to help you word your statement. The credit bureau must then include your 100-word statement in your report each time it sends it out.

Making Your Rights Work For You

Although most credit bureaus will be willing to work with you in resolving credit discrepancies, you need to remember they exist for the credit grantor more than they do for you. This will occasionally make the task of cleaning up your credit less than enjoyable. The best way to avoid running into problems is to be patient and cooperate with the bureau.

Another important point to keep in mind is that the rising number of "illegitimate" credit-repair companies has put most credit bureaus on alert. For this reason they may question your requests, especially if they feel your requests are frivolous or unwarranted. Once they realize that you are representing yourself, they should be more cooperative.

If you have been denied credit in the last 60 days, you should first draft a letter to the credit bureau listed on your rejection notice. In this letter simply state that you have been denied credit within the last 60-days. Also state that, as provided under the *Fair Credit Reporting Act*, you are aware that they must provide you, free of charge, with the information that led to the rejection.

The easiest way for the bureau to respond to your request is by sending you a copy of your report. If they choose not to send you a copy of your report, they still must respond and explain what information in your file led to the denial of the credit. To expedite the process, be sure to include with your correspondence a photocopy of the rejection notice, as well as a self-addressed, stamped envelope.

If you have not been denied credit in the last 60-days, simply contact the credit bureaus closest to you and find out if they have you in their files. When you do track down the bureau or bureaus that have your file, make an appointment to go in and look it over. Again, the fee will be around $15. Also, don't forget to contact the three major credit reporting agencies listed at the end of Chapter Seven. You will have to make your request to them in writing, as it will most likely be impossible for you to visit each one in person.

Chapter Seven

Cleaning Up Your Credit

*I have learned that success is to be measured
not so much by the position that one has reached,
as by the obstacles which are overcome while
trying to succeed. - Booker T. Washington*

Persistence, perseverance, and patience are the keys to success when it comes to cleaning up your credit. Remember, there are no magic formulas for erasing bad credit overnight, but with the *Fair Credit Reporting Act* backing you up, you shouldn't be forced to wait out the seven-year reporting period either.

The steps outlined in this chapter will show you exactly what you need to do as you embark on the task of cleaning up your credit report and negotiating with your creditors. The initial task is divided into two steps.

—Step One—

- The initial cleanup should deal strictly with items that simply do not belong in your report. Such items include mistakes dealing with your income, employer, marital status, etc.

Other items that should be taken care of in the initial cleanup include deleting items that do not pertain to you. Remember, with 170 million consumers on file, it is very likely someone else's information could erroneously show up on your report. Items such as these will be the easiest to cleanup.

The credit bureau can provide you with a form to dispute and delete any information that should not be attributed to you. If you subscribe to a credit bureau membership service, they will provide dispute forms in your membership package.

- Understand that outstanding debts do not necessarily constitute a negative credit rating. You can have a $100,000 debt load and still have a Triple-A rating. The only thing that will give you a negative rating is a history of past due payments, judgments against you, bankruptcy, tax liens, etc.

- The next step is to question any other inaccurate marks that appear on your credit report. For example, a delinquent bill may need to be updated to show that it is now current. You may find that the negative information has to be deleted simply because the bureau failed to reinvestigate or because the creditor did not respond to the investigation in time. (Although this does happen occasionally, despite what some credit-repair companies promise, you should not count on this method as a cure-all for negative marks on your credit report.) You may want to list each item being disputed separately to ensure equal and separate attention.

- Give the credit bureau the chance to work with you before you begin challenging it or quoting specific sections of the *Fair Credit Reporting Act*. You may find the bureau representatives to be very cooperative.

- Remember the *Fair Credit Reporting Act* requires the credit bureaus to act in a reasonable amount of time. Under most circumstances, 30 to 60 days would be considered more than reasonable. You may want to contact the credit bureau and ask how many working days it takes to process consumer disputes. Be persistent and demand that the credit bureaus honor your rights. Question any and all points or practices you feel are unfair.

- If you run into problems in your requests to have negative marks investigated, be sure to mention that your request should be deemed in order under Section 611 of the *Fair Credit Reporting Act* (Public Law 91-508). You may also find it necessary to send the request certified mail with a return receipt requested.

- When the credit bureau replies to your dispute, it should include an updated copy of your credit report. If it does not, be sure to contact the bureau immediately by mail and request that it do so. Once you have the updated report, look it over to see if you still have inaccurate marks on file. If you do, repeat the initial cleanup process one more time. If all the inaccuracies have been corrected, congratulations! You're done! Your efforts have paid off, and you can now begin concentrating on *enhancing* your credit profile.

By the way, don't get so caught up in the cleaning up process that you forget the other things you are doing to help you reach your financial goals. Each task should support the next, not detract from it. Also, it is crucial that you keep current on your Debt Elimination Plan as outlined in Chapter Three.

—Step Two—

The second step in cleaning up your credit report will shift from those items that are inaccurate to those that are accurate, but negative. There is little the credit bureaus can do to help you here so you will, instead, need to concentrate your attention on the actual creditors themselves. The steps you will need to take are as follows:

- You should contact each and every creditor that has given you a negative rating. If you know why you are being rated that way, do what the next step suggests. If you do not know why you are being rated negatively, find out.

- You need to explain that you are trying to mend your ways. Let the creditor know why you encountered the problem that led to your late payments or non-payments. Be honest with the creditor. If you were ill for six months with a rare disease brought to this country from Madagascar, say so. Or if you were called out of state to take care of your mother after a terrible accident involving a semi-truck and her little Volkswagen, tell the creditor. Be specific and to the point. But by the same token, if you were simply in over your head and did not have as much money coming in as you had bills to pay, tell the creditor that.

Tell the creditor you made some poor decisions and, at the time, the only way you could put food on the table was to skip payments on some of your bills. But don't embellish the truth. If the creditor feels you are making an honest effort to correct the situation you've gotten yourself into, he or she will most likely be sympathetic. Tell the truth. Nobody likes to be lied to or taken for a fool.

- Another important point worth making is that you should not give each of your creditors a different excuse. If you do, it will be obvious that you are just giving a lot of lip service but have not really changed your ways.

- If appropriate, be sure you include a statement in your credit report about why the non-payments or late payments occurred in case your creditors obtain a recent copy of your credit report. Remember, Section 611 of the *Fair Credit Reporting Act* allows you to place a 100-word statement explaining your side of the story.

"Even though you're in Debt . You are still a good person...with tatoos."

- Whatever you do, DO NOT become belligerent and unruly with the person you are talking to. Regardless of how inconsiderate they may be toward you, do not lose your cool. Remember, your creditors are your only hope when it comes to getting these negative marks erased without waiting seven years. Also realize that you may have to go through a number of people before you get to the one who can or will help you. The key is to be patient and to tell your story as many times as it takes.

- When you do find a sympathetic ear, ask for advice on what you can do to mend your relationship with the creditor and change the negative rating you are currently receiving. People love to give advice. They love to feel that they have something other people need. Go along with them, but at the same time, if something doesn't sound feasible, work with them to come up with a better solution or a compromise.

- You will most likely be able to work out a modified payment schedule that will be agreeable to you both. Don't think they can't lower your monthly payments. They can and will, if you explain your situation convincingly. Oftentimes, payment schedules can be stretched out a year or two longer than the original loan, thus making your monthly payments much smaller. At this point, pull out $5 or whatever you can afford and ask that it be applied to your next payment. This is a show of seriousness on your part and will most likely convince the person you are working with that you really have changed.

- Often, a creditor will grant you a moratorium as you try to get back on your feet. A moratorium is a reprieve for a specified time period during which you are not required to make any payments. After the reprieve expires, you begin making payments again. Or the creditor may allow you to make interest-only payments for a few months until you get back on your feet. Discuss these possibilities with your creditor.

- Regardless of how uncooperative or stubborn the creditor may be toward you, be sure to send something each month by way of a payment, even if it is only $5.

- During the negotiating process, make sure you get an agreement from the person helping you that they will see that your negative credit rating is erased and your account is updated with a positive rating. Be flexible and negotiate this point as well. It may take three or four months of regular payments before the creditors will agree to do this. Again, remind them that part of the reason you are even there talking to them is because you are trying to clean up your credit report and if you pay them what is owed, your rating should improve. You will find that most of your creditors will agree. Also, some of your creditors may have marked you off as a bad debt they never expected to receive payment on, so they will be thrilled when they find out you are going to come through after all.

- Don't attempt to negotiate over the phone. You can set up the appointment over the phone, but do the negotiating in person.

- "But I don't owe the creditors any more money, and they still have me rated negatively!" Well, the process is the same. Go to him, explain what happened and ask that they be sympathetic as you are trying to make up for some past mistakes. They have the power to change the rating on your credit report. If they refuse, wait a few months and go back and try again. You may find that persistence is the only way to accomplish your task.

• Another important point to keep in mind is that if your account has been turned over to a collection agency, the creditor has everything to gain by dealing directly with you. You see, collection agencies charge the creditors upwards of 50 percent on everything they collect. What this means is that there will be more room on the creditors' part for negotiations. For example, you could offer to pay the creditors 75 percent of what is owed, and they would still come out ahead. Remember, though, the creditors will be much more apt to change your negative rating if they get 100 percent of what is owed. Whatever the case, be sure to ask the creditors for their advice on what you should do.

• Before you leave the creditors' office, make sure you get the agreement and new terms of payment in writing. Be honest with them; tell them they are not the only creditor you are trying to work with and that a simple, written agreement will help you keep track of each of your debts. Include in the agreement that in return for your timely payments of whatever amount is agreed upon, the creditors will change your negative rating to a positive rating with the credit bureau.

• If you cannot get the creditors to agree to change your account to a positive

rating, settle for a non-rating. Anything is better than a negative rating.

• Finally, don't blow it again. Live up to your end of the agreement. If you find yourself running into difficulty—if you are sick, lose your job or something of the sort—contact the creditors immediately and explain the situation. Don't take it for granted that they will understand if you skip a payment one month. Contact them in advance and see if they will agree to a one-month temporary adjustment. Remember, though, that creditors, like anyone else, do not like to be taken for a ride. Don't push your luck, or you may find it running out.

If you find yourself with greater problems, such as judgments against you, foreclosures, bankruptcies, etc., you will most likely have to wait out the seven- to ten-year reporting period. But even still, don't give up hope. Be persistent, and most of all, be patient. Making your current debt payments in a timely manner will show that you are, once again, becoming a good "credit risk." A creditor may not hold the "old news" against you.

If you do find yourself waiting it out, by all means, do not let this deter or prevent you from achieving your goal of getting out of debt. Credit reports and getting out of debt, although related, are not tied to one another. You can have the dubious distinction of having the worst credit report on earth and still successfully eliminate all of your debts.

Fair Debt Collection Practices Act

If while traveling the road toward total debt elimination, you find yourself fighting

"It's not Death... it's Debt."

the infamous collection agency, you should be aware that you do have some protection under the *Fair Debt Collection Practices Act*. Most debt collectors are ethical and their contacts with you will be civil and reasonable. Nonetheless, there are some who seem to thrive on appearing as the black cloak, sickle, and kiss of death as they attempt to collect the "balance due." It is because of these back-alley debt collectors and collection agencies that the *Fair Debt Collection Practices Act* was passed in 1977.

The main purpose of this law is to protect you against abusive, unfair, or deceptive conduct by debt collectors. You are protected by this law whether you are in default on credit payments or not. The law does not, however, allow you to cancel legitimate debts that you owe.

Under this law, debt collectors may not use any false or deceptive tactics in order to collect a debt or obtain information. The following are examples of conduct forbidden by debt collectors when collecting debts:

1. Using a false name.

2. Pretending to be a government official, attorney, or credit bureau employee.

3. Falsely claiming that you have committed a crime and will be arrested.

4. Claiming that your property will be seized, unless it is legal to do so and the debt collector or creditor actually intends to do so.

5. Giving you papers that appear to be a government or legal document, but are not.

6. Leading you to believe that certain legal forms do not require any action on your part.

7. Giving, or threatening to give out, false information about you.

8. Threatening to take any action that cannot legally be taken or that the agency does not intend to take.

9. Continuing to contact you after you inform the collector that you wish it to cease communication or are being represented by an attorney. (A sample letter is provided in Appendix C to request that the creditor cease contacting you.) At this point, the collector can only contact you to acknowledge receipt of your request or to inform you of legal action to be filed against you.

10. A debt collector is forbidden to make any kind of contact with you before 8 a.m. and after 9 p.m.

11. A debt collector is forbidden to contact you at any unusual place or time. An example would be when carrying your groceries to your car.

12. Collectors are forbidden to contact third parties, such as employers, friends, family members, or neighbors to collect a debt. They may, however, contact third parties for the purpose of learning your address, phone number, or place of employment. Debt collectors may not, however, state to the third party that they are a debt collector or that you owe a debt. Nor can they contact the

third party more than once without their permission.

13. The debt collector may not publish or print your name in any form relating to the debt or on a list of consumers who refuse to pay their debts. (This includes the list of "bad check writers" you've seen at your local grocery checkout stand.) Nor may they communicate with you by way of post card.

14. The collection agency cannot force you to pay for any communication with them, be it telegram, collect phone call, etc.

Furthermore, the *Fair Debt Collection Practices Act* specifically prohibits collectors from harassing, threatening, or in any way abusing consumers. This prohibition includes, but is not limited to:

1. The use or threat of violence.

2. The use of obscene or profane language.

3. The use of telephone calls in which the caller does not identify himself or herself or intends to annoy any person in your household.

If you feel you have been abused by a debt collector or if you feel a debt collector has broken the law, you have the right to file suit in a federal or state court within one year after the law was allegedly broken. You are entitled to recover the amount of any actual damages, as well as court costs and attorney's fees. A judge may also award you up to $1,000 in additional damages. The Federal Trade Commission has primary responsibility for enforcing the *Fair Debt Collection Practices Act*. The address is:

Division of Credit Practices
Federal Trade Commission
Washington, D.C. 20580
(202) 724-1140

It may also be helpful to contact your local consumer protection agency or your state Attorney General's office. You may also want to consider contacting an attorney.

And For Further Assistance?

If you find yourself needing further assistance or counseling with your debts or payment schedules while cleaning up your credit, try contacting the Consumer Credit Counseling Service (CCCS). This is not one of the fly-by-night credit repair agencies referred to earlier, but rather a non-profit organization that counsels consumers who have substantial debt. The CCCS has over 280 offices nationwide. Their counselors will try to help you arrange a repayment plan that is acceptable to you and your creditors. They will also help you set up a realistic budget and plan expenditures. These counseling offices, which are funded by credit-granting institutions, are offered at little or no cost to consumers. You can find the CCCS office nearest you in the White Pages of your telephone directory or by sending a self-addressed, stamped envelope to:

National Foundation for Consumer Credit
8701 Georgia Avenue, Suite 507
Silver Spring, Maryland 20910
(301) 589-5600

In addition, non-profit counseling programs are sometimes operated by universities, military bases, credit unions, and housing authorities. They are likely to charge very little if anything at all for their assistance. Or you can check with your local bank or consumer protection office to see if it has a listing of reputable, low-cost financial counseling services.

The addresses of the nation's three largest credit bureaus and the address for TRW Credentials Service referred to in Chapter Six are listed below:

TRW
P.O. Box 2350
Chatsworth, California 91313-2350
800-392-1122 or 214-235-1200

Equifax
P.O. Box 740241
Atlanta, Georgia 30374-0241
800-685-1111 or 404-885-8000

Trans Union Corporation
P.O. Box 7000
North Olmsted, Ohio 44070
313-689-3888

TRW CREDENTIALS service
P.O. Box 14008
Orange, California 92613-1408
800-262-7432

Chapter Eight

Taming the Monster

Success is a journey, not a destination.
- Ben Sweetland

As you well know, the age in which we live is an age of credit. Like it or not, chances are you will never have the things you desire, or be able to do the things you want, unless you have a clean credit report and, to go along with it, adequate credit limits. In the previous two chapters we discussed how to get copies of and clean up your credit report, and how to negotiate with your creditors. In this chapter, we will focus not on the credit report, but on the credit instruments themselves. "But credit has destroyed me," you cry. "Shouldn't I just stay away from it altogether?"

First of all, credit has not destroyed you. If you still have breath entering your lungs and blood flowing through your veins, you are not destroyed. And the key is not to run and hide from the animal that haunts you, but rather to face it, take hold of it, and tame it to be your ally. But any animal trainer will tell you that, before you can tame or train something, you have to develop a positive working relationship with it.

If you don't believe credit is necessary to get by in today's world, try testing the system. Try qualifying to buy a home or an investment property to enhance your financial portfolio. If you do not have adequate credit, you will find it almost impossible to do either of these, or anything else that will move you forward and improve your position in life. The purpose of this chapter is to introduce you to the proper use of credit. We will discuss the various forms of credit available, how to get credit even if your credit history is not what it should be, and, finally, what to do with the credit once you have it.

"But I thought you were going to tell me to cut up all my credit cards!" Of course you did. Practically every credit repair company or self-help program you encounter will have as its primary ingredient the destruction of your credit cards and the severance of your relationships with every one of your creditors. My advice to you is **not** to cut up those cards! The purpose of this program is not to make your life miserable or inconvenient, but rather to teach you, step-by-step, how to manage your financial affairs successfully. Cutting up those credit cards for some, in fact, would be nothing short of copping out. My philosophy is that it simply takes too long to establish and build up your credit to watch it go up in smoke or fall to the ground with the slice of the sewing scissors.

The ultimate goal, again, is to have your credit and credit cards working in your favor. To do this you will obviously need a system that will help you manage your credit and finances and enhance your credit position while not adding anything more to your debt load.

The system has already been developed and is right here in your hands. The purpose of this chapter, and the chapter that follows, will be to introduce you, or at least reacquaint you, with the various types of credit available and teach you how to manage your credit successfully.

Still not convinced that you need credit to get along?

Let me relate a story that will help you better understand the importance of credit. An acquaintance of mine, Jay, had the dubious pleasure of receiving a substantial inheritance from a relative in the form of stock. Although the will divided the stock equally amongst a number of children and grandchildren, Jay's share was still quite large. He did what many would consider the appropriate thing to do. He left the majority of the stock in place to supplement his income with the dividends it paid. The rest he cashed in. As many of us would do, he used the proceeds to buy a nice car, a Porsche in Jay's case. He also bought a motorcycle and a second, smaller car just to get around in.

Not satisfied with the fast toys, Jay decided to invest part of the money in real estate. He bought a three bedroom home, complete with a basement that he could rent out to college students. Of course, he paid cash for everything.

Then came more toys! He added televisions, VCRs, entertainment centers, mountain bikes, video cameras, and so on and so on. There's no sad ending to the story. Jay still has all of his toys. He has the house paid for, free and clear. But what he does not have is a credit history. You see, he paid cash for everything. "Who cares!" you say? "He has everything he could ever want and doesn't owe anyone any money!"

Well, eventually Jay decided to use his video equipment and his degree in Broadcast Journalism to start his own video production company. His money, however, was mostly depleted, with the exception of the stock he was living off. So he went to the local bank to get a small business loan. As he sat across from the loan officer, he never thought he would hear the words that came out of her mouth:

"I'm sorry, sir, your files show that you are not a good credit risk."

"That's crazy," he replied, "look at my assets!"

"I'm sorry, sir, you've never purchased anything on credit, so we have no way of knowing if you'll ever pay us back."

Quite upset at this point, he asked the loan officer, "Do you own the home you live in free and clear?"

"No," was her reply.

"Do you own two cars, one of them a Porsche, free and clear?"

"No."

"Do you have enough stock on the New York Stock Exchange to ensure your standard of living for the next several years?"

Of course, again the reply was "No."

The logic just doesn't seem to be there, does it?

Well, to make a long story short, Jay never got the loan. The purpose of sharing this experience is not to make anyone feel sorry for Jay; to the contrary. In fact, most of us would give our right arm to have half the things Jay has free and clear.

The point of the story is to illustrate the fact that it doesn't matter who you are or what you have, if you don't have adequate credit, you are at a serious disadvantage in today's world.

If you do not yet have credit, this chapter will help you as you set out to establish it. If you do have credit, this chapter should help you determine if you have the right types of credit and if you have enough of it. If, on the other hand, your credit profile is right where you think it should be, this chapter will hopefully spark in you the motivation, not to keep it where it is, but to continually fine tune it to help you go even further toward reaching your desired goals in life. Before we get into what credit is right and what credit is wrong, and how much is too much or too little, let's answer some of the basic questions that often come up when dealing with credit and credit cards.

The Most Commonly Asked Questions

What is credit? The simplest answer is, buying now and paying later. Credit permits you to obtain something now for little or no money out of your pocket, and pay for it over a specific period of time. Today, almost everyone uses credit in one form or another. Mortgages, credit cards, personal loans, and car loans are all types of credit.

What is open end credit? Open end credit is credit which is extended on an ongoing basis, but usually with a limit on how much you may borrow. It is often referred to as revolving credit in that as you repay the balance due, credit up to a specified limit is then available to you again to use at any time in the future. The most common forms of open end credit are credit cards, such as VISA and MasterCard.

What is closed end credit? Closed end credit is credit that is extended on a one-time, limited basis, such as a car loan or a personal loan. Although you may still have a positive relationship with the lender after paying off the obligation, you still must requalify each and every time you want another loan.

Who extends credit? Credit is most frequently extended by department stores, finance companies, oil companies, credit unions, commercial banks, and credit card companies. Those who extend credit are called creditors.

How can I get credit? For credit to be extended to you, you have to be someone who a creditor considers to be a good credit risk, or "credit-worthy."

What does credit-worthy mean? A credit-worthy consumer is someone who the creditor believes can repay the amount borrowed over a certain period of time. This ability to repay is often judged on the basis of a credit scoring system.

What are credit scoring systems? Credit scoring systems are systems that try to predict whether you will meet your financial obligations and make regular payments on your bills. These systems consider various factors such as income, length of time on the job, length of time at one residence, previous credit history, amount of debts outstanding, stability of

your checking and savings accounts, number of dependents, and so on. Each creditor has different ways of evaluating applications, so do not be discouraged if one creditor turns you down. Other creditors may be willing to grant you credit.

How do I prove myself credit-worthy and meet the standards of a credit scoring system if I have never had credit before? First, open a checking account, savings account, or both. Then apply for credit gradually through retail store credit cards, a major bank credit card, or a gasoline credit card, if you believe your budget can handle the financial load. Don't apply for more credit than you can manage. A credit card establishes you with credit as soon as your application has been approved.

You can prove your credit-worthiness by making regular payments for the products or services you purchase. Every time you make a payment to a creditor, you are building a favorable credit history. If you consistently repay your debts, your credit history should be favorable. Should you fail to repay the credit extended, however, you will establish a poor credit history, which may result in future credit applications being denied.

If I have never had credit before and don't have a credit history, can I get credit with a co-signer? In some cases credit may be extended to you if you have a responsible person with a good credit history who is willing to act as your co-signer. A co-signer is a person who guarantees payment of the debt. This protects the creditor by reducing the risks involved in extending you credit. Whoever co-signs for your credit is responsible for repaying your debt should you fail to do so.

If you successfully repay a debt on which you have a co-signer, it indicates to the creditor your willingness to repay credit and your ability to responsibly handle debt. This helps in establishing a good credit history. Failing to repay a co-signed debt, however, will add to a poor credit history, not to mention what it will do to your relationship with the co-signer.

How can I tell how much credit I can afford? A good way to determine how much credit you can handle is by making a household budget. A budget is composed of nothing more than a listing of your income and your expenses. Charts for figuring your budget are provided in Chapter Nine. If you find that you cannot afford credit purchases, considering your current income and current expenses, you should still concentrate on establishing

good credit, but continue making your purchases using cash. (Refer to *The Spending Plan* in Chapter Nine.)

Credit Cards

It is important to realize that all credit cards are not alike, nor will every type of credit card suit your particular situation as you set out to establish and enhance your credit profile. The various types of credit cards include "bank" cards such as VISA and MasterCard, travel and entertainment cards such as American Express and Diner's Club, department store cards such as JCPenney and Sears, and gasoline cards such as Exxon or Texaco. In addition to these commonly used credit cards, there are a variety of other "credit" cards that are rapidly becoming popular. Discover Card, a subsidiary of Sears, is a good example.

You should also be aware that there are a number of lesser known companies that

If I get caught I can always chew my arm off.

purport to have "credit" cards that are easy to get and guaranteed without a credit check. Be aware that despite what the advertisements say, most of these lesser known cards are not widely accepted and can often cause more pain than pleasure when it comes to enhancing your credit profile. If you have a question about any card or credit device being advertised, consult with your local Better Business Bureau or Consumer Protection Agency. If the card or company cannot be verified as legitimate, STAY AWAY!

A good rule of thumb is simply to stick with legitimate and recognized credit card companies. Although the "Neapolitan" card may purport to offer all the same services for a mere 5% interest, you will likely find that the actual service and safety of the card will not live up to its promises. Besides, a potential lender will be much more impressed to see a VISA, Exxon, or American Express account on your credit report than he will the "Neapolitan" card.

Each of the legitimate cards mentioned above are very similar and work in about the same way, meaning they can be used to buy now and pay later. And although there are literally thousands of banks across the country that offer their own bank cards, almost without fail, each of these cards will be a VISA or MasterCard. Although they all carry the same name, they are unrelated when it comes to issuance and billing. For this reason there is nothing stopping you from having several VISAs and MasterCards, all from different banks around the country.

How is it that all of these banks can offer the same card but still be independent of one another? Well, in the mid-1960s, Bank of America in California began selling BankAmericard franchises to other banks throughout the country. BankAmerica's (now referred to as VISA) success was so phenomenal that four other California banks decided to join together and start their own credit cards to be franchised out as well. The result, the "Interbank Card" now known as MasterCard, gained immediate popularity and continues today to rival VISA for the spot as the industry leader.

Today, banks throughout the country continue to use VISA and MasterCard franchises and put their own bank names on the cards they offer to their customers. These bank and other credit cards are normally accepted worldwide in virtually every type of business establishment you run into, be it a restaurant, hotel, motel, retail outlet, gas station, etc. Also with bank cards, regardless of whether they be VISA or MasterCard, the financial institution or bank that issues the card is responsible to see that payments are made for the purchases you charge on the card. Practically every bank credit card will fall under the category of revolving credit cards mentioned earlier.

Major department stores like JCPenney and Sears normally issue revolving credit cards as well. Department store cards, however, usually can only be used at outlets of the store chain that issued the card.

Gasoline or oil company cards are issued for the purchase of goods or services at that company's service stations. They may also have arrangements to be used at certain hotels and motels.

Travel and entertainment cards (like American Express) can also be used at a wide variety of places throughout the world and may entitle you to additional services like travel insurance, discount mail order services, and travelers checks. Many VISA and MasterCard issuers are now offering these benefits as well. An advantage to travel and entertainment cards is that they will normally have higher credit limits than other credit cards. The catch is that you are almost always required to pay the entire balance due at the end of each month. Travel and entertainment cards, along with many of your bank cards, also carry annual membership fees. Most department store and gasoline credit cards do not.

Annual membership fees are relatively easy to understand. They are nothing more than another way for the creditor to make another dollar off the consumer. You see, as the credit revolution unfolded, consumers began to get wise. They figured out that if they paid their balance in full at the end of each month, there would be no interest charge. The only problem with this is that the interest charged is the lender's profit. If everyone did this the lenders would be providing a nice service, but simply wouldn't make any money. For this reason, creditors began charging membership fees of $20, $30, $50 or more. Now, even if you do pay off the balance at the end of each month, the creditor is still assured of making a profit. Never fear, though, there are still bank cards available with no annual fees. In fact, stiffer competition and an increase in the number of companies offering credit cards is causing many lenders to drop their annual fees to entice customers. In September 1992, *USA Today* reported that of the 2,000 institutions issuing credit cards, nearly one-fourth had already dropped or waived their annual fees. Addresses of some of the banks offering these cards are provided at the end of Chapter Ten.

"The serpent gave me a credit card."

So what of the stiffer competition? In the late 1980s and early 1990s many companies besides banks began introducing their own VISAs, MasterCards, and various other credit cards. Among those taking a piece of the plastic pie and increasing the credit competition; AT&T, GTE, General Motors and General Electric. How have they done? Well, you decide. The AT&T Universal MasterCard and VISA pulled in over 10 million customers in its first two years. That's an average of over 300,000 new accounts each month. General Motors with its "no annual fee" and "5% rebate on GM car purchases" MasterCard signed up over one million new customers in less than 30 days after introducing its card in late 1992. In fact, Associated Credit Bureaus, Inc., estimates that over 950 million credit cards are in use in America today.

More Questions and Answers Concerning Credit and Credit Cards

Who can apply for a credit card?
Anyone can apply for a credit card as long as the individual is old enough to enter into a legal contract according to the laws of the state where the application is made.

Where can I apply for a credit card?
Credit card applications are distributed in many of the places where cards are accepted, such as department stores, drug stores or other retail outlets. Application forms are also available from the bank, financial institution, or company that is issuing the credit.

Are some credit cards easier to get than others?
Yes. Obtaining a credit card from a merchant may be easier than obtaining a credit card from a bank or other financial institution. Merchants' standards for granting credit are usually not as strict as financial institutions'. If you want to apply for a credit card from a financial institution, it may help to apply where you have an account or have previously received a loan.

Once I get a credit card, how will it work?
When purchasing items in a department store, you present your credit card to the merchant, and a record is made of the purchase. You will then receive a monthly statement from the card issuer, listing the purchases, payments or returns that you made during the billing period. The statement also will show the total amount that you owe or any overpayments that you made, which result in a credit on your account.

How much credit will I be allowed?
Credit card companies generally limit the amount of credit that you are given based on your income as well as other factors. For example, if you make $10,000 a year, a major bank credit card company might limit your spending to $300 when you are first accepted. After proving yourself credit-worthy by making regular payments, the limit may be raised to $700 or more. Each creditor will have its own standards for granting credit.

And remember, while two financial institutions may offer the same bank or credit card, the terms of the card (credit limit, interest or annual fee) may not be the same. It pays to shop around for the best terms available, just as you would for the best deal on an automobile.

Will I have to pay for all of my credit purchases as soon as I receive my bill? No, not always. As was mentioned earlier, credit cards are also called revolving charge accounts and offer you a payment-plan choice. You may pay the balance of the monthly charges in full or in smaller payments, whichever fits your budget. The exception is travel and entertainment cards, which usually require payment in full each month. Just be careful not to accumulate debt you can't handle.

As was mentioned earlier, another advantage of a revolving credit account is that in many cases the use of the credit is free as long as you pay the full amount you owe before the finance charge is computed. A wise shopper can actually have free credit for almost two months if purchases are carefully timed. For example, let's assume that your billing date is the 25th of every month. If you charge a shirt on March 28, it probably won't appear on your billing statement until April 25. If your payment is due in 25 days, you will have until May 20 to pay for the shirt you bought on March 28. Because of this "loophole," many creditors are beginning to impose minimum finance charges, or have their finance charges begin on the day you buy the item, and thus you get no *free* credit.

What is a finance charge? A finance charge is the amount of interest you have to pay on the unpaid balance of your account. The interest rate or finance charge varies from state to state and from creditor to creditor. Again, shop around.

What is an annual percentage rate? The annual percentage rate (or APR) is the cost of credit expressed as a yearly rate. It is the key to the cost of the money you borrow. If one credit card carries a 15% APR and another an 18% APR, and if all other terms are the same, the finance charges on the 15% APR card will cost you less than the card with an 18% APR.

How Potential Creditors or Lenders Look at You

As you become familiar with the basics of credit cards, don't forget that there are other instruments of credit as well. Of course the most traditional way to get credit would be to apply for a loan at your local bank. If you are qualified and have a good relationship with the bank, you may be able to get what is called a signature loan, which is nothing more than a loan backed up by your promise to repay. This is the riskiest type of loan for the lender because he has nothing more than your word that you will repay the obligation.

Another type of loan available is the ever-popular secured loan. A secured loan simply means you put up collateral of equal or greater value than the amount being borrowed to ensure the lender that he will have something of value that he can take if you fail to make your payments as agreed to. You don't actually give the lender the item being pledged as collateral, just the right to come in and take it if you fail to live up to your end of the obligation. A good example of a secured loan is a car loan. The bank doesn't actually keep the car—only the title. That way if you fail to make your payments, the bank, being the legal holder of the title, can come in, take your car, and sell it to get the money you owe. If, on the other hand, you do pay off the loan, the bank will then send you the title and you become the legal owner of the car. (Of course, by this time the car is usually five years old and it's time to buy another car.)

The third most common type of loan is the co-signed loan. A co-signer is simply someone with good credit who agrees to affix his or her name to the loan along with yours. By doing this, the co-signer agrees to pay the balance in full if you fail to do so. This is usually the easiest type of a loan to get. The only hard part is convincing somebody to co-sign for you. Banks are comfortable with this type of set-up because if you fall through on your payments or declare bankruptcy, they have someone else they can legally go after to get what is owed them.

Will You And Can You?

Regardless of whether you are applying for a credit card or a loan at a major bank, your ability to get the credit will depend on two main factors: your *willingness* to repay and your *ability* to repay.

For a creditor to determine your willingness to repay, he need only look at your credit report. If your credit report has too many negative marks or not enough positive marks, he will most likely shy away from extending you any credit at all. Be aware, though, that your willingness to repay can be relayed to the lender in ways other than just what is found on your credit report.

For example, how you deliver and "sell" yourself to the loan officer is very important. The key here is to dress for success. The man in the white shirt and tie or the woman in the pressed skirt and blouse will make a much better impression than the one in blue jeans and a tee-shirt. Who would you rather lend your money to, the person who appears respectful and on the ball, or the person who appears disrespectful and out on bail? Remember, in today's world, what other people think about you is important. This is especially true if the person doing the judging is the one who will determine whether you are going to get something you really need or really want. Go out of your way to make sure you are well groomed and well mannered before you enter the loan manager's office.

References are also very important. Anyone who cannot provide the lender with at least three or four character references will automatically raise a few red flags. Also, be sure to contact in advance anyone you plan to use as a reference. Don't risk having someone say something negative about you. Check with those you want to use as references and make sure they will say what you need them to say. If they won't, find a legitimate acquaintance who will.

Be aware also, that even if you do provide the potential lender with solid references and even if you dress to the hilt, if your credit report is not up to par, you will most likely find yourself fighting an uphill battle. If you find yourself in this position, the first thing you should do is go back to Chapter Seven and clean-up your credit report. Besides, if you have negative marks on your credit file, you should be concentrating on eliminating them before you try to get more credit!

In addition to your *willingness* to repay, potential lenders will also be looking at your *ability* to repay the obligation. Of course, a dead giveaway will be your income. If you make under $12,000 per year, or under $1,000 per month, most creditors will not grant you credit because it likely takes every penny of your income just to pay your basic living expenses: food, shelter, clothing, etc. But depending on your monthly expenses and your current debt load, some creditors may give you a token credit limit of $200 or $300 even if your income is low.

Another important factor in determining your ability to repay is the stability of your income. This is determined by the source of your income and by how long you have been relying on it.

For example, if you have been with the same employer for three to five years, most creditors will view this as satisfactory. Anything less than this will cause lenders to question.

Also, if your employment is seasonal, like construction work, or if your income is from self-employment, you will most likely find yourself at a disadvantage. (If you are self-employed, you will need to provide tax returns for the past couple of years or some other proof of your income.)

As potential creditors look further into the possibility of lending you money or extending you credit, they will also be looking at your income to debt ratio. An acceptable ratio will normally run between 20% and 25%.

"Debt? Hey, in this baby you can outrun it."

For example, if your annual income is $20,000 after taxes, the debt load that would be considered acceptable would be about 25% or $5,000. Thus, if you already have credit limits totaling $3,000, the lender will most likely not feel comfortable extending you more than an additional $2,000.

One of the last factors that will determine whether you are deemed a good credit risk will be the score you receive on the lender's credit-scoring system. If you score high enough, your application will most likely be accepted. If you do not score high enough ... need I say more?

Some of the things that may be considered on the creditor's score card, or items that may be considered as reason to reject a credit application are:

— Credit application incomplete
— Insufficient credit references
— Unable to verify employment
— Temporary or irregular employment
— Length of employment
— Insufficient income
— Unable to verify income
— Excessive obligations
— Delinquent credit obligations
— Not at current residence long enough
— Inadequate collateral
— Temporary residence
— Unable to verify residence
— No credit file
— Insufficient credit file
— Garnishment, attachment, foreclosure, repossession, or suit
— Bankruptcy
— Too many inquiries into your credit report
— Lack of stability in savings/checking accounts

— No telephone listed in your name
— No savings or checking account with the lending institution
— Credit is not granted to any applicant on the terms and conditions you requested

This list is obviously not complete. Each institution will have other items on their score cards; others may not use a scoring system at all. But for those that do, a typical rating system will probably run similar to this:

0-40 percent of possible points: Reject outright! This application is for the circular file.

40-50 percent of possible points: Review with great caution, leaning toward rejection unless something really extraordinary surfaces.

50-70 percent of possible points: Review carefully but leaning toward approval.

70-90 percent of possible points: Grant the loan unless red flags appear that cannot be explained.

90-100 percent of possible points: Grant the loan!

Most consumers will fall in the middle category with 50 to 70 percent of the points possible. A full credit review will normally accompany such an application. Those falling into lower categories, on the other hand, will probably have to revert to the secured loan or co-signed loan. Those in the higher categories will most likely be considered very good credit risks and will be granted credit on their signatures alone.

If You Have Been Denied Credit

If you have been denied credit, find out why. Under the *Equal Credit Opportunity Act* (ECOA), you are guaranteed the right to know the specific reason or reasons for denial of credit. It may be that the creditor thinks you have requested more money than you can repay on your income. It may be because you have a poor earnings record, a late or past due payment record, or that you have not been at your current residence for an acceptable length of time. Whatever the case, the ECOA states that you must be given the specific reason for rejection of your application.

The creditor, however, may not offer the reason or reasons for rejection unless you specifically ask. If you do ask, the creditor has no choice but to tell you. To get a written statement of the reasons, you must make your request in writing within 30 days of the time you were informed of the lender's decision. The lender then has 30 days in which to respond. But regardless of whether you ask for a written statement, you should still feel free to discuss with the lender any questions you may have about your application and about the lender's decision.

If you think that you have been discriminated against or that the lender refused to grant you credit without a viable reason, you may contact a federal enforcement agency for assistance or you may bring legal action against the lender.

The ECOA provides such legal remedies for unlawful acts of discrimination. Courts may, in fact, award actual damages and in some circumstances may impose punitive damages against the lender of up to $10,000. If your lawsuit is successful, the court can also award court costs and attorney's fees.

Who Do I Complain To?

If you have a complaint about a bank in connection with any of the federal credit laws or if you think any part of your business with a bank has been handled in an unfair or deceptive way, you may get advice and help from the Federal Reserve. You should submit your complaint in writing to:

Director of the Division of Consumer and
Community Affairs
Board of Governors of the Federal
Reserve System
Washington, D.C. 20551

Be sure to describe the bank practice to which you object and give the name and address of the bank involved. The Federal Reserve normally will respond within 15 days.

Now that you are up on the various forms of credit available, you need to spend some time evaluating your current credit situation and then decide what types of credit will best help you meet your future goals. (This is dealt with in Chapter Nine). Bear in mind that what may be the "right" credit for one person may not necessarily be right for another.

As you learn how to use credit to your advantage, it will then become like a chisel molding your financial future, instead of like a sledge hammer destroying your financial dreams.

Chapter Nine

Enhancing Your Credit Profile

If you don't want to work, you have to
work to earn enough money so that you
don't have to work. -Ogden Nash

Any soldier will tell you that before going into a combat situation it is wise to find out who the ally is, who the enemy is, and to be able distinguish between the two. You would then, of course, try to use the ally as an aide in accomplishing the task at hand, and try to avoid or eliminate the enemy.

This is the task at hand: your own personal war on debt is being waged. Some forms of credit are the enemies and others are the allies. You will have to determine which is which. Be aware that fighting a battle does not mean you always have to be on the offensive, looking for trouble. In fact, the ideal situation in this

credit war is to be on the defensive—protecting what is yours, enhancing and fortifying it as you go.

Defusing The Bomb

A wallet or purse packed full of credit cards is nothing more than a time-bomb waiting to go off. Thus, the first thing you need to do is defuse your bomb. Take all the cards you are carrying, and I do mean **ALL** the cards—charge and credit cards alike—tie them together with a rubber band and then put them in the bottom of your sock drawer or in another safe place—but not on your person.

"Okay," you say. "I'll do that tonight when I go upstairs." WRONG! Do it right now. Get up, go get your purse, wallet, briefcase, or whatever, and lay those cards to rest. They will come into play at a later date, but for now put them away for your own safety. (By the way, don't keep them in the kitchen junk drawer. They are too easy to get to there, too easy to misplace, and too many people have access to them there.)

It is not necessary to go out and get a safety deposit box or anything like that ... just put them somewhere where you won't have to worry about them. Some, however, may find that the only way to keep from using their cards *is* to lock them away in a safety deposit box. If you lack the self-control to keep your cards in their proper place, the deposit box may be your best bet.

I've even heard of some people who have to get two safety deposit boxes at different banks at opposite ends of the city. They put all of their credit and charge cards in one box at the first bank and put the key to that box in another box at the second bank.

Now with your bomb defused, commit to yourself once again that you will not incur another dollar of debt for the rest of the day. Remember to take things one day at a time. If there is something you need, pay cash for it. If you do not have cash, write out a check or go to the bank and get cash. "But that is such an inconvenience," you say. Of course it is. That is the whole idea. Credit and charge cards are <u>too</u> convenient for us. That is why so many people owe their creditors so much money.

You might even want to do what I do and not even carry cash. I carry a checkbook. I find cash too easy to spend, and because many places won't take a check, I am limited in what I can spend on any given day. This scares my wife, and she is always slipping $5 into my wallet just in case what she calls "an emergency" arises. That's okay, too, but I've never once used that $5 for an emergency. Maybe one day I will, but so far I've spent it on soft drinks, frozen yogurt (black raspberry), magazines, or whatever else seemed necessary at the time. You'll have to decide what method of payment is best for you, but whatever it is—cash or check—DO NOT buy anything on credit ... at least for now.

"What about my gas cards?" you ask. "It's stupid to have to pay cash for gas, right? Gas is something I've got to have. Can't I just make this one exception and pay for it all at once at the end of the month?" The answer to that is a resounding NO! If you make an exception for the gas cards, you will do the same with American Express and then JCPenney and then one of your VISAs, and before you know it, the only thing in your drawer will be your socks!

You can always rationalize the fact that if you're going to buy it anyway, you may as well put it on the card, defer the payment and then pay the bill in full as soon as it comes. Don't fool yourself. Excuses will only get you deeper and deeper into debt. Don't get blown up by your own bomb.

There will be some temporary inconveniences, but they will pass and life will be sweeter tomorrow. Every task is much easier to accomplish when tackled little by little, day by day.

"But how can I enhance my credit profile when all of my credit is hidden away between my socks?" Be patient and remember the motto, "Step by step, little by little." Enhancing your credit profile will come as each step falls into place. In the meantime, you can be sure those credit and charge cards will not be destroying your credit profile any further.

Your Personal Credit Profile

Understand that although very similar, your credit profile and your credit report are not the same thing. As was explained in Chapter Six, your credit report is a tangible piece of paper that rates the payment track record on each of your debts, past and present. Your credit profile, on the other hand, is not a tangible piece of paper, but rather it is the personality, so to speak, of the credit available to you.

Thus, the second step to enhancing your credit (after the sock drawer) is to determine what your current personality or profile is saying about you. To do this, identify *what* types of credit you currently have and then decide if these are the *right* types of credit.

If you do not have any charge cards, credit cards, loans, etc., this does not mean you have no personality, but rather that your credit profile is still in its infancy.

If you do have credit, you need to identify it on paper. Use the form on page 106 to do this. Fill in every column

except for the last. It will be explained later in the chapter.

Once you have everything identified on paper, you can then go back and determine whether each item is a positive addition to your credit profile or a negative one.

It could very well be that every ounce of credit you have will be positive and that all you really need is the right plan and training to teach you how to use it more effectively. Whatever the case, use the form provided and let your personality come through on paper. (The Target computer software can print forms for your credit profile.)

Include on this list anything that would be considered a reportable item to a credit bureau. For example, personal loans from friends or family would not need to be listed. Credit cards, charge cards, department store cards, gas and oil cards, bank loans, special lines of credit at your local bank, etc., should be included.

Fill in the appropriate column next to each item. If a column does not apply, write N/A for "Not Applicable."

If you are not sure what the grace period, annual fee, or interest rate is, call the lending institution or look at the original documentation that came with the card or loan.

"Secured" simply asks whether you had to put up any collateral to get the loan. For example, did the bank take your car title, a work of art, a piece of jewelry, or something else of value to ensure that you would pay back the loan?

PERSONAL CREDIT PROFILE

#	Creditor/Lender	Credit Limit	Interest Rate	Annual Fee	Grace Period	Secured Yes/No	Equity Built Up	Rating +/-/?
1								
2								
3								
4								
5								
6								
7								
8								
9								
10								
11								
12								
13								
14								
15								
16								
17								
18								
19								
20								
21								
22								
23								
24								
25								
26								
27								
28								
Totals			N/A		N/A	N/A		N/A

The "Equity" column will most likely only apply to real estate like the home you live in. Automobiles, for the most part, depreciate and would not have equity building up. The "+/-/?" column is so you can go back later and rate each item as to whether it is good, bad or indifferent to your credit profile. After filling out the form provided, you may want to place a copy of it in your personal folder.

The ideal credit profile or personality will be the one with the lowest interest rates, no annual fees or at least the lowest possible annual fees, the longest grace periods, a comfortable credit limit and no collateral or security deposit tied up. And although it is possible that you could have all of this in your favor now, it will most likely take a little time before you get to that point.

You can now go back and rate each of the credit instruments on your list. To do this all you need to do is look at each of the columns and determine if the credit is helping you or hurting you. Understand that at this point we do not care how much you owe on each credit instrument, only what its personality or makeup is like.

For example, if you have an unsecured VISA or MasterCard with a $1,000 credit limit, no annual fee, 13.9% interest and a 25-day grace period, this would be a big plus! The credit limit is reasonable. There is no annual fee, thus the card will not cost you anything if you decide not to use it. The interest rate is reasonable compared to what other cards might cost you. And if you do use the card, you won't pay interest if you pay the bill within the 25-day grace period. If you could have fifteen of these,

you would be in great shape! Of course, if you had fifteen of these and racked them all up to the limit, you would be in pretty sad shape. *The Spending Plan* explained later will teach you how to avoid getting into that predicament.

Let's look at a different scenario. Let's say you've got a VISA or MasterCard, still unsecured, but this one has a $300 spending limit at 21% interest and an annual fee of $20. The grace period is the same as the previous card, 25-days. This would have to fall into the (-) or negative category. Why? Well to begin with, the costs associated with the card are too high in comparison to the credit limit. The interest rate, for example, is extremely high.

"But if I pay the balance due when I get the bill, I won't pay any interest." Yes, that is true, but if, on the other hand, you do not pay the balance due, you are going to be penalized to the tune of 21%. Even if you tuck the card away and don't use it at all, you are still going to pay $20 a year in annual fees just for the privilege of having it. If you could have the first card we discussed, why would you take the second?

Case three: Let's say you have a JCPenney card with no annual fee, 18.9% interest, and a 25-day grace period. This would fall into the (?) or indifferent category. It will look good on your credit report if your payments are kept current, but at the same time it doesn't really provide you with much spending power. You see, the only place you can use it is at JCPenney. If you need to get $500 in quick cash, tough luck!

Okay, let's make it a little more difficult. You have a MasterCard Gold with a $5,000 credit limit. The interest rate is 18.9% and the annual fee is $35. The grace period is the same 25-days. Depending on your particular situation, this could go either way. In most cases this would probably be a (+) or positive credit instrument because even though it is costing $35 a year just to have the card, the higher credit limit can justify the annual fee. Besides that, a $5,000 credit limit will be a great boon when it comes to convincing other creditors that you are a good risk. Once you have proven yourself, if one creditor thinks you are worth the $5,000, others will likely follow suit.

On the other hand, if you're only making $8,000 per year and you've got a card with a $5,000 limit, you could find yourself in a fix. What if you charged it to the limit? Big trouble, huh? Another thing to take into consideration is that with only $8,000 income and a $5,000 credit limit few, if any, other creditors are going to give you credit for fear you are already in over your head.

Charge cards like American Express will also have different personalities for different individuals. "The Card," as they call it, has tremendous buying power, is accepted worldwide and is very prestigious. It definitely would not hurt to have this one as part of your credit profile. The drawback is that the American Express card is not like a traditional revolving credit card, but instead is a charge card with its balance due in full when you get the bill. Of course there are no interest charges when you pay your bill in this manner. The annual fee, however, is quite a bit higher than most other cards.

The last time I checked, the fees were $55 for the Green Card, $75 for the Gold Card and $300 a year for the Platinum card. A pretty hefty sum if you're in debt, but very convenient and prestigious if you can afford it.

Gas and oil cards normally do not have annual fees and work much like department store cards. These would be indifferent, or a "?," on your "Personal Credit Profile" chart.

Bank loans are normally pluses because as you make payments and eventually pay the loans off, they will show up as positives on your credit report. Annual fees are normally non-existent, and interest rates on bank loans will be relatively reasonable when compared to credit card rates. Besides, if the interest rate is too high, you can always refinance. As was explained in Chapter Four, refinancing simply means you get a loan with a lower interest rate and pay off the loan with the higher rate.

Unless the equity on your real estate holdings is negative, real estate will usually be considered a plus. If, down the road, you need to use the equity as collateral for a loan, you have it. Real estate normally appreciates in value, thus helping your financial portfolio and net worth as well.

Although the examples listed here are meant to serve as a guide, you need to keep in mind that these are only examples. Each item on your own credit profile will be unique to your individual situation.

You will have to make the judgement call as to whether a particular item is positive, negative or indifferent. The only guideline I can give you is to be honest with yourself. Don't let pride or the false power credit provides govern the decisions you make.

Once you have rated each item, the weeding out needs to take place. Put in the simplest terms, the credit instruments with the negative ratings need to be eliminated. To do this, contact the creditor and explain that you are canceling the card. If they ask why, tell them the truth. The interest rate is too high, you have other cards without annual fees or the credit limit is too low so there is no need to keep their card.

Most creditors will tell you to cut the card in two and send it to them. Whatever you do, after canceling the card, DO NOT make any charges on it. If you do, you will get in serious trouble with the law and wreak havoc on your credit report. Once it is canceled, it is no longer your card.

Doing Whatever It Takes

While eliminating those items that are not enhancing your credit profile, don't forget the main reason you're reading this book: to help you get out of debt and to put your other financial affairs in order. Remember the commitments you have made to yourself. Remember the goals you plan to accomplish over the next six months, the next year, the next five and ten years. Take a moment now to look back at your goals and recommit to do whatever it takes to accomplish these goals.

Sadly, the majority of the people who buy this book will follow almost every step exactly as outlined, with the exception of the one we are talking about now—destroying and canceling any credit or charge cards that are not enhancing their credit profile.

"I am the exception," they say. "My credit cards have the potential to enhance,

if I learn to use them correctly." They try to fool themselves by compromising and making excuses like these:

- I can control my spending, if I really want to.

- It took too long to get the card; I can't just kiss it goodbye.

- I'm a salesman, and I need it to entertain customers.

- I'm a doctor; I need the prestige that comes with the card.

- I'm a lawyer.

- I'm a dentist.

- I travel too much to totally rely on cash.

- I didn't have a problem with the card until now; I'm sure things will change.

- I'm no worse off than anyone else.

- It's so convenient.

- What would my mother-in-law say?

- The country club doesn't take checks.

- I've paid my dues.

- I work 16 hours a day and commute an hour each way; I deserve this.

- I need the credit card to rent a car.

- It's necessary to cash a check.

- I need it for identification.

- My wife wouldn't understand.

- What if an emergency came up?

- I can't do this to my family.

- Christmas is too close.

- It would interfere with our vacation plans.

- I would feel naked if I didn't at least have it with me.

The list goes on and on, and so does the debt. But excuses will not pay the bills. Nor will excuses help you sleep any better when the bills begin to pile up. Remember, you do not need to cut up all of your credit cards, only the ones that qualify as negatives on your "Personal Credit Profile" chart. No one should be a slave to anyone or anything, especially to a 2 x 3 inch piece of plastic. Put away the excuses. Take charge of your own life.

Dealing With The Positive

Once you have eliminated all the credit instruments that are not enhancing your credit profile, you can begin concentrating on, and enhancing, the ones you rated as positive. To do this, determine if the credit limit is substantial enough to be of benefit to you. If the limit is considerably low, contact the creditor and ask that the limit be raised. If you have consistently paid your bills and have not fallen behind in any of your payments, most of your creditors will grant you at least a token increase. If they will not, ask them what you need to do to qualify for a higher limit, then try to meet their requirements.

"Oh no, I think we just made an unnecessary expense."

If, on the other hand, you feel your credit limits are realistic right where they are, there is no reason to ask for more. Enhancing your credit profile does not necessarily mean you have to have more, more, more, or that you have to have outrageously high credit limits. It simply means you need to use the credit that you do have to its fullest potential.

If, after eliminating all of your negative credit instruments, you find you have little or no plastic left to your name, never fear. In the next chapter you will learn how to obtain credit and charge cards with relatively low interest rates and no annual fees.

As you are doing all of this, don't forget to continue following the other steps outlined in the previous chapters.

Continue working on the other goals on your list. If, for example, one of your goals is to become an expert on Renaissance Art, be sure to take time to go to the library to study the great masters.

Let the steps in this guide and the goals on your list complement one another. And most importantly, concentrate on your "Debt Elimination Schedule."

The Spending Plan

Continuing with the commitment not to incur a single dollar of debt for the entire day, you are now prepared to put into action *The Spending Plan*. Like the other steps in this book, *The Spending Plan* contains no hidden secrets—only logical, practical, common sense guidelines that, if followed, will work.

The first step in *The Spending Plan* is to keep a record of every expense you incur each and every day. This may take a little time and a little practice to get used to, but it *will* be worth it.

To keep this record, you will obviously need to carry around a piece of paper and something to write with. Some find a daily planner works well. For others, this is a little awkward. Women who carry a purse will have no problem, and most men can keep the paper in their wallet and the pen in their coat or shirt pocket. The important thing isn't *how* you keep track, but rather *that* you keep track of each and every penny.

When you get home each night, transfer the record of that day's purchases to your personal file, or binder. Keep a running total for each day of the week. Here is what an average day might look like.

Tues. Feb. 11th

Newspaper . . .	.55
Donut/milk . . .	1.25
Bus	.90
Lunch	4.69
Taxi	5.16
Shoestrings . . .	1.10
Gum	.62
Flowers	<u>22.50</u>
Total	$36.77

Now tomorrow you probably won't buy flowers and shoestrings again so it is likely you won't spend as much either. Some days you will spend more, especially on the weekends when you take the family shopping or to dinner or something of the

sort. Whatever the case, be sure to keep a meticulous record of each and every penny.

After doing this for a week or so (it takes about a week to determine how much you spend on an average day) you need to start making a budget for each day. The purpose of this budget is to help you set a limit, or at least, a target amount that you would like to keep your spending under for the day.

If you know a large purchase is going to take place on that day, budget it in. Sticking to your budget will help you eliminate many of your impulse purchases. The forms on the next page can be photocopied to keep track of your daily expenses. Additional Daily Expense forms are in Appendix B.

If you see a trend of unnecessary spending over a period of time, be sure to eliminate it. For example, if you are spending $50 a week on lunches, you may find it necessary to brown-bag it two or three days a week. You'll be amazed at how much money you can save when you keep track of where it is all going.

If you see something you really want or a deal you just can't pass up, but you're maxed out for the day, there is some flexibility to this plan. (Of course the best thing to do is to pass it up ... besides in a couple of hours you will probably be glad you didn't buy it.) If you do run across something that you absolutely must have, and if it's something you can afford ... buy it. But wait a day or two before you do so. Figure it into tomorrow's budget or next week's or next month's. By doing this you will have more time to think about

The Spending Plan
Daily Expense Forms

Daily Expenses	Date:
Item	Cost
	Total

Daily Expenses	Date:
Item	Cost
	Total

Daily Expenses	Date:
Item	Cost
	Total

Daily Expenses	Date:
Item	Cost
	Total

the purchase, and to determine whether you really need it and whether you can really afford it. Granted, an occasional "splurge" will not kill anyone. The only problem here is that you will have to use a tremendous amount of self-control to keep from compromising your way into unnecessary purchases every day of the week. By the way, when I use the term "splurge," I am referring to flowers for that someone special, not a BMW!

It might also be a good idea to implement what I call the "Seven-Day Rule." The Seven-Day Rule applies particularly to major purchases but can also be applied to smaller ones. The way it works is simple. If you see something you want or think you need, do not buy it until you have waited seven days. By doing this, you will likely talk yourself out of the purchase before the week is up, or you might even find the item at a better price some place else.

Remember though, when you do make a purchase, write it down. Don't think you can rely on receipts (or your memory) and then log your purchases at the end of the day. One reason is that the hot dog vender on the street probably does not give receipts. The other is that even if he does, you probably will not remember to ask for one. Write down each purchase immediately and transfer it to your master record in your financial folder at the end of each day.

At the end of each week, review how you did. Determine what unnecessary purchases took place, what you need to improve on, and what things fell into place as scheduled. Remember, as you are making these everyday purchases, pay

cash. Do not incur a single dollar of debt during the day!

If you follow the spending plan as outlined, you will never again be baffled as to where the $30 in your wallet went.

More On Budgets

As long as we are talking about spending plans, records, and budgets, it only makes sense to mention the need to budget your personal finances on a monthly basis as well. If you do this, your daily and weekly budgeting or record keeping will be much easier. Use the Budget Chart provided on the next page. (There are extras in Appendix B.) You may want to make a few copies of the budget chart to keep in your folder for future months as well. The Target computer software referred to throughout this book will also help you track your monthly budgets.

The easiest way to figure your monthly budget is to start at the beginning of the month. Add up your income: your salary, your spouse's salary, and any other money you will receive for the month. Enter the sum in the "Total Income" column under the "Amount Estimated".

Then make a list of your estimated fixed and variable expenses. Fixed expenses are things that are constant, like rent, automobile insurance, etc. Variable expenses are the expenses that change from month to month, like the phone bill, electricity, groceries, etc. Add the sum of all of your estimated or anticipated expenses and enter the number next to "Total Expense" under the "Amount Estimated" column.

MONTHLY BUDGET

	Month _____			Month _____		
	Amount Estimated	Amount Spent	Difference	Amount Estimated	Amount Spent	Difference
Rent/Mortgage						
Phone						
Utilities						
Groceries						
Dining Out						
Clothing						
Auto Repairs						
Gas and oil						
Parking/tolls						
Bus and taxi						
Credit Card 1						
Credit Card 2						
Credit Card 3						
Auto Loan						
Personal Loan 1						
Personal Loan 2						
Student Loan						
Other Loan 1						
Other Loan 2						
Life Insurance						
Health Insurance						
Property Ins.						
Auto Insurance						
Disability Ins.						
Tuition/Fees						
Books						
Medical/Dental						
Child Care						
Recreation						
Emergency Fund						
Savings						
IRAs						
Investments						
Gifts						
Miscellaneous						
Total Income:						
Total Expenses:						
Difference:						

Calculate the difference between the two. (You may end up with a negative number and have to adjust some of your variable expenses.) Then at the end of the month, go through your daily and weekly records to determine the exact amount spent for each expense and calculate how close you came to your budget.

For some people, budgeting can be quite an enjoyable experience. For others, it will be something dreaded each and every day, each and every month. Whatever the case, budgeting is the best way to keep track of where your money is going as well as where you may need to cut back.

Credit And The Spending Plan

So you're thinking the record keeping makes sense, but what about all those credit cards tucked away in the sock drawer? Well, once you have mastered the daily record keeping outlined in *The Spending Plan* and are sure you can keep with it, then you are ready to move on to the next step, *Credit And The Spending Plan.*

The way this works is simple. All you need is a checkbook and a credit card. Which credit card? The one with the lowest credit limit. Why? Insurance against having a hot flash and buying that BMW on your credit card. If you want to use your gas card or your JCPenney Card that is fine. Just make sure you keep it to one card and one card only.

"Okay, I'm armed with my checkbook and one credit card. What next?" Well, you still need to pay cash for all of your *minor* purchases. But for other purchases you can use the credit card. The only catch is that you also must use your checkbook for the <u>same</u> purchase. No, you don't pay for it twice. You simply make out the check at the time of the purchase

for the amount of the purchase and place it in a special envelope or keep it in your checkbook. Deduct the amount of the check from the balance in your checkbook and then pay for the item with the credit card. When the credit card bill comes at the end of the month, use the check you wrote earlier to pay the bill. The amount due should be the same as the amount on the check, and since you already deducted it from your checking balance, there are no surprises.

Oftentimes you will have several checks made out to one creditor. This would happen, for example, if you had been using your gas card. If this is the case, simply add all the checks together, make out a new check for the combined amount, and mail it with the statement. Be sure to void and destroy all the others checks so you don't get confused as to whether you paid the bill.

A tremendous amount of self-control is <u>crucial</u> when following this plan. For example, you must have money in your checkbook when you make the purchase, or the plan simply will not work. Do not fall into the trap of overextending yourself. If next Friday is payday and you don't have the money in your checkbook to cover a purchase today, you <u>ABSOLUTELY</u> must wait until Friday to make the purchase. If you do not, life's unexpectancies will overtake you and will ultimately destroy your plan of paying off your debts.

"Why bother with the credit card if I still have to write out a check? Doesn't this defeat the whole idea of having a credit card?" Well, yes and no. It does defeat the idea that credit cards are for

your convenience, but convenience is not your goal. Your goal is credit enhancement and debt elimination. And the only way to enhance your credit is to use your credit.

You see, a charge card never used will simply show up as an inactive line of credit. This will not help you enhance your credit profile, nor will it help you if you ever need to get more credit. Why would a creditor give you an increased limit if you never use the credit you already have? As you use the credit and pay the bills when they come due, your credit profile will begin to shine, and you will have a Triple-A rating and a dynamic "Personal Credit Profile" before you know it.

In order to give all your credit instruments equal enhancement opportunities, it will be necessary to rotate cards from time to time. After using one card for a month or two, put it back in the drawer and use another card for the next few months. Be sure to keep a record of which card is being used each month.

Do this again and again with each of your credit and bank cards. But only carry one at a time. Remember, a wallet or purse chock-full of credit and charge cards is a time-bomb just waiting to go off!

By only charging items your checkbook will cover and by writing out the check at the time of the purchase, you will never again have to wonder whether you will have enough money to pay the bill when it comes. You will have already paid it. All you need to do now is send off the check!

Of course the <u>best</u> way to enhance your credit is to continue making regular monthly payments on your home, car, and any other outstanding loans you may have. You do not have to go out and get more, more, more in order to enhance your credit. All you have to do is take care of the credit you currently have in an honorable and timely fashion. As you do so, your credit profile will be greatly enhanced and so will the lines of credit available to you. And as you consistently make your payments in full and on time, you will soon find yourself swamped with credit applications for other cards with higher credit limits and lower annual fees. When these begin to roll in, you can then re-evaluate your current credit profile, your current debt situation, and your current credit needs, and make any changes you feel are justified.

The Ideal Situation

There really is no such thing as the "ideal situation." What may be right for one person will be totally wrong for another. The best way to determine what is right for you is to spend some time really examining your current credit profile. Decide once and for all if each credit instrument is really necessary or if it will just add to the debt load that is currently weighing you down. If it is necessary, learn to tame it and to use it to your advantage. If it is not necessary (as is the case more times than not), get rid of it!

As I have met and dealt with people from every possible financial background, I have come to the conclusion that credit and charge cards are no more good than they are bad, and no more bad than they are good. Only you can decide what is right for you as you strive for total debt elimination.

CAUTION: If you are currently in over your head, it would probably be a good idea to keep the number of cards you have to a bare minimum. Remember, if you pay with cash, you will not go further into debt.

Most will find that one gasoline card, like Exxon or Texaco: one travel and entertainment card, like American Express and one VISA or MasterCard, to be used only in emergencies or in conjunction with your checkbook will be more than enough. Practically every department store will take VISA and MasterCard, thus eliminating the need for a wallet full of department store cards.

Defuse the bomb, be realistic about your credit needs, and follow the steps outlined in these chapters and you will join the ranks of those who have taken charge of their lives and reached the heights of success and freedom.

The Last Resort

Some of you will find that the only way you can concentrate all of your efforts on your debt elimination is to get rid of all of your credit and charge cards once and for all. If you, or your spouse, lack the self-control to follow *The Spending Plan* to the letter, you may be better off without your credit cards. Yes, this is ... "The Last Resort."

The simple fact is that despite the oppressive disgust that accompanies the bills each and every month, some of us still cannot seem to get the spending out of our system. We try and try, but still we always find some reason or excuse to "charge it" just this one last time. Compulsive debtors or spenders are much like the chain smoker who says, "I can quit anytime, I've quit three times this month already." For these compulsive spenders or compulsive debtors, the only way debt elimination will ever become a reality is first to eliminate the credit and charge cards.

The sock drawer has failed. The safety deposit box has failed. The time has come to, once and for all, take control of your life. Get out the sewing scissors, cut up those cards, and send them back to your creditors.

"But, but, but you said I could keep the cards." I know what I said, but for some of you, there simply is no alternative. If you are one of the thousands who has tried in the past to put an end to the charging but consistently seem to fail, you <u>must</u> take that painful and final step and eliminate the monster that is making your life so difficult. Look at it like this: cutting up the credit cards is guaranteed to work! If you don't have them, you can't charge with them.

"But what about enhancing my credit? What about the credit profiles and credit reports we've been talking about?" Priorities, my friend! The number one priority on the list has got to be <u>eliminating</u> <u>your</u> <u>debts</u> so you can begin to enjoy your hard earned money rather than being a slave to your creditors.

"But I don't think I can do it." Well, you simply must! If after you accomplish your goal of getting out of debt, you decide you want to make a go of it again, you may. Just start out small, with a $300 credit limit or so. Be sure to follow *The Spending Plan* as outlined, and you will see how quickly your credit begins to improve and enhance itself.

But for the time being, if you lack self-control, you must learn to live without the credit and charge cards. If you do not, it is almost guaranteed that you will fail.

Why all this negative talk all of a sudden? It's not negative, it's reality. If you think you can make a go of it if you really work hard, then try it. People can change. Perhaps by following *The Spending Plan* you will be able to change your ways. But if you are deep in debt and have failed in the past, do yourself and your family a favor. Cut, cut ... snip, snip.

You are not alone. Do not think for one minute that you are the only one who ever had to cut up his or her credit cards. Thousands before you have reverted to this last resort ... and thousands after you will do so as well. But again, think about the bright side of what many consider a painful situation; it really works!

If you decide to take this route, it does not mean you have failed. In fact, just the opposite is true. You have merely taken a different approach than some of the others toward reaching your goals. You are to be congratulated for mustering up the courage, the willpower, and the determination necessary to become the master of your own destiny.

Chapter Ten

No Credit? No Problem!

In all labor there is profit.
-Proverbs

The very fact that you are reading this book makes the likelihood that you do not have any credit extremely low. After all, for most of us, it would have been difficult to get into debt to begin with if we did not have at least some credit. Nonetheless, for those of you with no credit, for those whose credit is the wrong type, and for those needing to start over, this chapter is for you.

First Things First

Before you set out to establish yourself in the world of credit, you need to establish yourself with a financial institution by opening a checking account and/or savings account. Most financial institutions will do this with a minimum deposit of around $5. Those just starting out may want to use a credit union. Credit unions offer a wide variety of services and generally will cater to those with little or no financial and credit experience. Banks are okay, but my personal preference is the credit union. (More on banks and credit unions later in the chapter.) The only thing you need to look for in a bank is that it offers a VISA or MasterCard with a reasonable interest rate, grace period, and annual fee.

If you already have a bank or credit union, you will probably be better off dealing with it. If, however, you have had problems with your bank or have continually been overdrawn in your checking account, you may find it necessary to start out fresh with a different lending institution.

Although you can open an account at most institutions for around $5, be aware that when potential creditors check into your account, they will be told the amount of the initial deposit, so it helps to make this deposit as large as possible. It might be a good idea to borrow the money to open the account from your parents or a good friend and then pay them back from the new account immediately. As you become more established, creditors will be able to find out more about your average monthly balances, etc. But for now, make the initial deposit as large as possible.

After you have the account, or as you are opening it, apply for the bank's VISA or MasterCard. Many banks will require you to make a savings deposit as security against the card, but this is okay. It's still your money; all it does is assure the bank that its money will be repaid if you fail to come through on your payments. Many institutions will set up an equal security deposit, meaning if you deposit $500, your credit limit will be $500. Others will have you deposit a percentage of your credit limit, usually between 50 percent and 75 percent.

Still others will not require a security deposit at all, but will prefer a co-signer. It is usually best to use a relative, although a friend or acquaintance will do. If you can get by without a co-signer and without a security deposit, that is great. Chances are that if you are just starting out, your credit limit will be low, around $300 or so, but that is still a good start. As you prove to the bank that you are conscientious and reliable, your limit will go up.

Credit Applications

If you have no credit or if you are re-establishing your credit-worthiness, you will likely be filling out a number of applications over the next few weeks and months. As you do this, it will become very important that all of the information is consistent from application to application. The easiest way to maintain this consistency is to create a master credit application. This way you will not have to struggle to remember what you wrote on the last application. There is no special form for this master application. All you need to do is use a credit card application from any bank as your master form. Write across the top in big red letters—"Master Application"—fill it out and place it in your binder or folder for future reference.

Most people think that if they keep their applications honest, there will be no need for this master application. But regardless of how truthful you may be, the need still exists. The reason is that applications do not ask for every aspect of your life or every item of credit ever extended to you. They only ask for certain information, much of which can be worded in a variety of ways. The key is to give the same information to each creditor. That way all of your bases will be covered, and you will not find yourself explaining why you wrote one thing on one application and something else on another.

Keep in mind the credit scoring system when filling out applications as well. Often they will only ask about one or two credit or department store cards. Which will you put down? If you are smart, you will put down the ones that will flatter your application rather than shadow it. Also, keep in mind the point system that you are up against. You need to carefully examine every item of information on your master application and make sure it sheds as much positive light as is truthfully possible. If you have a VISA card with a $300 limit and you have never missed a payment and you have a MasterCard with a $5000 limit and you have consistently missed payments, which would be the better reference? The VISA of course. A couple of other points you need to keep in mind:

- Keep it honest. To knowingly make false representations on an application for credit constitutes fraud. And fraud is a criminal offense.

- Always type your application. Try to be as professional as possible. Of course you will not be able to fill out the application on the spot, but the extra time it takes to go home or to a friend's house to type it will pay off down the road. (This is true regardless of what type of application you are dealing with, be it credit, employment or otherwise.)

- Fill in every space on the application. If a particular space doesn't apply to you, write N/A for not applicable.

Developing Strong Bank Relationships

As you learned in the chapter on cleaning up your credit, it is extremely important to develop a strong relationship with the bank's loan officer. Set up an appointment to meet with him or her. Explain your situation; that you are just starting out and that you are interested in any advice he or she may have for you. Chances are the advice will be good. If it is, follow it. Be sure to get the loan officer's business card for future contacts.

When you get home, write the loan officer a quick thank-you note for his time. Then periodically, if you are cashing a check or if you are conveniently in the neighborhood, pop your head in to say hi ... and let the loan officer know how things are going. Keep your visits short (do not take too much time by sitting down—remember you were just passing through), and always keep your visits positive. (By all means, if you just lost your job, do not share that! Instead, you could say that things are really looking up and that you are in the process of looking into some greater employment opportunities that could really help you accomplish some of the goals you discussed earlier.)

Be prepared for questions that the loan officer may throw at you, but remember to keep the visit short and sweet. If he or she invites you to sit down, say you would like to but that you really are in a hurry—you just wanted to say hello and say thanks again for all the help.

Do not wait too long after your initial visit before you stop by the second time. If you do, it is likely he or she will not remember you. As you develop your relationship with the loan officer, you will find your financial opportunities and horizons really beginning to expand. Don't go about this with the attitude that you are using the bank officer. If you do, it will show through and backfire on you. Be sincere. Really go out of your way to develop a genuine relationship. You never know, this person may become one of your best friends or personal references down the road.

It is also important to be realistic and understand that not every bank officer is going to be a nice person. Some will be cold and rude. Don't let them get to you. Be honest with them, and they will most likely soften up. If they do not, you don't need to give them your business. Go across the street to the competition.

Credit Unions

I mentioned at the beginning of this chapter that credit unions are my personal favorite, as far as financial institutions go. Understand that because *I* like them does not mean they will necessarily be best for *you*. The services, personnel, and facilities banks have to work with can make them extremely enticing.

I, on the other hand, prefer credit unions because they are just the opposite of these large conglomerates. I like the personal service and low overhead. I feel they understand me and want to help me work out my financial future. Banks, on the other hand, have a tendency to treat their customers as account numbers rather than individuals. But again, you may not find this to be true at your bank. Whatever the case, here's a little history on credit unions.

Probably the easiest way to explain what a credit union is, is to explain what a credit union is not. Many people, for one reason or another, simply do not understand what credit unions are or what they do.

• Credit unions are not part of an organized labor union.

• Credit unions are not banks or finance companies.

• Credit unions are not collection agencies or credit counseling centers.

Credit unions, on the other hand, are nonprofit organizations made up of individuals with some sort of a common bond. They may all work at the same place, go to the same college, or live in the same neighborhood. Maybe their children all go to schools in the same district.

Whatever the case, members of a credit union will normally have a common tie that brings them together.

Credit unions, as we know them today, have actually been in existence in the United States since the early 1900s. When they first came into being, their main goal was to help the poor. Often they were organized by churches or neighborhoods aiming to help members get low cost banking and loan services. That aim, for the most part, has continued to the present.

Although many credit unions have quite elaborate set-ups, for the most part, overhead will be kept to a minimum. The lack of marble counters and brass fixtures means savings are passed on to you.

Loans are much easier to get through credit unions because, as a member, you are actually a "part-owner." Credit unions will normally give very small loans as well, something most banks will not do. Interest rates on loans are usually lower than you would find at conventional banks, and most credit unions offer credit cards, VISA or MasterCard, and normally at better rates than do most banks. Some credit unions have even begun offering larger loans like home mortgages.

"What do you mean I'm a 'part-owner'?" Well, to join a credit union you are required to buy at least one share of stock at a cost of $5. That $5 is deposited in your savings account. As a member you are then entitled to the checking, savings, and loan services offered by the credit union. As a member you are also eligible to elect the officers that actually run the credit union and make managerial decisions. You will be notified of upcoming elections and be given candidate information by mail.

Many credit unions also offer special services to their members such as low-cost health insurance, life insurance, and travel and shopping discounts.

Not every town will have a credit union. The easiest way to tell if yours does is to look in the yellow pages under "Banks," "Credit Unions," or "Financial Institutions." Call those listed and ask what the requirements are to join. Some credit unions only have a few hundred members. Others, like military credit unions, may have hundreds of thousands of members.

Again, a credit union may not be the way for *you* to go, but it definitely will not hurt to check it out.

Debit Cards

Relatively new to some parts of the country, but old news in other parts, is the debit card. How the debit card works is simple. It will normally be a VISA or MasterCard, thus offering wide acceptance virtually anywhere you go, but charges made on the card are automatically charged against your checking account. Thus if you decide to put that new popcorn popper on your debit card, you won't get a bill at the end of the month, rather the charge will be deducted from your checking balance. This is a great convenience! The only thing you need to be careful of is that you deduct the charge from your checking balance as soon as you make it. Otherwise, you will find yourself overdrawn.

Department Store Credit

Once you have a VISA or MasterCard, obtaining a department store credit card is

much easier. A good rule of thumb is to apply at stores where you are likely to shop. If there is no JCPenney in your town or state but there is a Montgomery Ward, go for the Ward's card. Inactive accounts will do nothing for your credit profile. Also remember that as you begin to get these credit and charge cards, you must follow the spending plan exactly as outlined in the previous chapter. Otherwise, you will find yourself so deep in debt that the only solution will be to cut up those cards you worked so hard to get. And in the meantime you will have destroyed your credit rating.

Again, the purpose of charge and credit cards is not to get into debt, but rather to enhance your credit profile as well as the credit related opportunities waiting for you.

Establishing Quick Credit

Although applying for, and getting, credit and charge cards takes time, it can still be worth the effort. And once you have established yourself as credit-wise, you will soon find your mailbox full of credit card and loan applications.

Obviously, you do not need to get every card or loan offered you, but, instead, should only apply for those cards and loans that will enhance your credit profile. Remember that the return must be greater than the investment, so don't apply for every card under the sun. Qualify each potential lender and decide whether each card or loan will be a plus or a minus on your "Personal Credit Profile." If it will be a minus, or if you simply do not need more credit at this time, file the application away for the future or toss it altogether.

In addition to credit and charge cards, there are other ways to establish good

credit. Probably the easiest way is the "Rotating Bank Method." Many self-help and how-to books offer this same idea disguised under different names. Whatever it is called, the goal is still the same ... to establish a Triple-A credit rating in a minimal amount of time.

It will normally take about six months before this method will pay off for you but, if followed and managed correctly, it will pay off. And best of all, it does not cost you anything but a little time to fill out the paperwork and juggle the payments.

This is how it works: Go to any bank in town and open up a regular savings account with a deposit of $500. You will want to wait about three business days for the account to be posted before proceeding. Then, go back to the same bank and apply for a $500 loan amortized over 12 months. Offer your savings account as collateral. If

you do this, most banks will not even do a credit check.

Take the money from that $500 loan and go to a second bank in town. At this bank do the same thing. Deposit the money in a savings account. Three days later, apply for a $500 loan secured by your savings. Do this again at a third bank.

Finally, go to a fourth bank and open a Checking Account. Deposit the $500 loan from the third bank into this checking account. BE SURE TO KEEP THIS CHECKING ACCOUNT SEPARATE FROM YOUR PERSONAL CHECKING ACCOUNT. You will not want the two of these combined.

Wait about one week and then make one monthly payment on each of the three loans out of your checking account. Wait about two weeks and make another monthly payment, out of checking, on each of the three loans.

In a very short time period, your credit report will show that you not only have an active checking account and adequate savings, but that you are also regular, even ahead on your monthly payments to your creditors.

After you make a couple of payments on each loan you will have freed-up equal amounts of money from your savings accounts. You can then withdraw that money from savings and deposit it in your checking account to make your upcoming payments.

Continue doing this until all of the loans are paid off. You will have to absorb the interest charges, but on $500 the interest should not be too high, most likely not more than a couple of dollars a month. Also, keep in mind that you will be receiving some interest on your savings accounts.

Make two payments on each loan every month, and in six months you will have established a 12-payment credit history on three loans.

After you have completed the repayment process, the most important step still needs to be carried out. Luckily, it's also the easiest step. You need to contact each of the creditors you had loans with and request that they report your loan details to the credit bureau they subscribe to as well as the principal credit bureau you are dealing with. If you have made your payments on time, your creditors will be more than happy to do this for you. And when they do report, your credit profile will be in A+ condition.

Other Possible Sources of Credit

In your efforts to mold your credit profile don't be discouraged, as you will inevitably run into snags and delays. Remember, patience is a virtue! If, after checking with all the local banks and credit unions, you still have not found anyone that will give you a credit card or at least a credit card with reasonable rates, the list of banks on page 128 may be of help. Most of these institutions will offer credit cards to all areas of the country and likewise, most of these have extremely low interest rates (as low as 8% as of the printing of this book) and low or no annual fees.

Two other sources that will be of help as you search for these low interest rate and low annual fee credit cards are CardTrak and Bankcard Holders of America. Both offer lists, for a reasonable fee, of banks and lending institutions issuing these cards. In fact, CardTrak estimates that there are currently over 450 cards now offering rates under 15 percent.

CardTrak will sell you its Credit Card Newsletter with a list of 500 bargain credit cards for only $5. Bankcard Holders of America offers an updated list of 50 banks with low rates and/or no annual fees. The cost for their service is only $4.

CardTrak
P.O. Box 1700
Frederick, Maryland 21702
800-344-7714

Bankcard Holders of America
460 Spring Park Place, Suite 1000
Herndon, Virginia 22070
800-327-7300

Institution	Address	Phone
AFBA Industrial Bank	909 North Washington Street Alexandria, Virginia 22314	800-776-2322
Amalgamated Trust & Savings Bank	Box A-3979 Chicago, Illinois 60690-9983	800-365-6464
Arkansas Federal Savings Bank	P.O. Box 8208 Little Rock, Arkansas 72221	800-477-3348
Astoria Federal Savings	One Wall Street Oneonta, New York 13820	800-752-8406
Bank of Montana	P.O. Box 5023 Great Falls, Montana 59403	800-735-5536
Bank of New York	P.O. Box 6999 Newark, Delaware 19714	800-942-1977
County Bank	419 Main Street Greenwood, South Carolina 29646	803-229-2551
Dauphin Deposit Bank & Trust	P.O. Box 4332 Harrisburg, Pennsylvania 17111	717-255-2339
First Columbus National Bank	710 Main Street Columbus, Mississippi 39801	601-328-7932
First National/St. Mary	1100 Brashear Avenue Morgan City, Louisiana 70381	504-385-0330
First State Bank	P.O. Box 910 Malta, Montana 58538	406-654-2340
Home National	126 South Summit Arkansas City, Kansas 67005	316-442-4040
Mechanics Bank	3170 Hilltop Mall Road Richmond, California 94801	415-262-7200
NCNB Texas Credit Card Services	411 North Akard, P.O. Box 830411 Dallas, Texas 75283-0411	800-548-2959
Oak Brook Bank	P.O. Box 5033 Oak Brook, Illinois 60522	800-666-1011
The Abbott Bank	10040 Regency Circle, Ste. 300 Omaha, Nebraska 68114	800-999-6977
USAA Federal Savings Bank	P.O. Box 21658 Tulsa, Oklahoma 74121	800-922-9092
Wachovia Bank Card Services	77 Reads Way, Commons Blvd. New Castle, Delaware 19720	800-842-3262

Secured Credit Cards

If you still find yourself running into problems because of a bad credit report, no credit, bankruptcy, a charge-off or other credit-related problems, there is still hope. As was mentioned earlier, most banks offer secured credit cards. Often you can even determine your own credit limit by the amount you deposit in a savings account at the issuing bank. If none of the banks in your area offer secured credit cards, you may want to try the two listed below.

First Consumers National Bank
Lincoln Center Tower
10260 SW Greenburg Rd. Suite 600
Portland, Oregon 97223

Service One Corp.
26660 Agoura Rd.
Calabasas, California 91302
(818) 880-5191

A Time To Save

There is a basic law governing personal finance. It is this: in order to get ahead financially, you have to bring in more money than you spend. There is another basic law governing your financial future: if you don't plan now, you will be sorry later.

When it comes to savings, most Americans have the same strategy. Spend first and then save whatever is left over. The only problem with this strategy is that it doesn't work. Most of us will always be able to find a new expense to cover any additional money we might have. The answer, of course, is to save first and spend later.

Before we get further into the various savings techniques, keep in mind what we talked about back in Chapter Three. If you owe a lot of money, you cannot afford to be putting money in savings earning 5% or even 10% while you're paying 22% on your debts. Follow the strategy outlined earlier. Keep enough in savings to live on for about three months and use the rest to pay toward debt.

At this point, we are assuming your debt load has become manageable and that you are in a position to begin putting something away for the future. There are a number of ways to begin this savings process.

Many financial planners agree that a good way to budget your money is to pay yourself first. The way you do this quite simple. Each time you get a paycheck or receive income from any other source, take a certain percentage of the money and put it in a savings account. Do this before you pay any bills or before making any other payments or purchases. A good rule of thumb is to save 10% of your take-home pay each year. If saving 10% is too ambitious considering your other obligations, try saving a smaller percentage. Maybe 3% or 5% is a good start. Then as your income increases or as you pay off more of your debts and other obligations, continue to increase your savings until it reaches the 10% mark.

Many banks and credit unions will help you in your efforts to save by automatically deducting a set amount out of your paycheck or checking account each month and applying it toward a savings account. This can often be as effective as the forced savings you receive through an insurance policy. Ask your bank about automatic transfers.

Another good rule of thumb is to always deposit in savings any money you receive unexpectedly. For example, if you receive money as a gift for a birthday or if you get a nice Christmas bonus at work, that is normally money you would not have been counting on to pay bills. The short answer ... Save It! Another good way to save a little extra is to have a savings jar at home. Have everyone throw their extra change in the jar. When the jar gets full, deposit it in the bank. This is a great way to encourage family members to save for a vacation or another special purchase.

You should also make full use of any savings or pension plans offered through your work. Financial analysts estimate 24 million employees are eligible to participate in 401(k) savings plans or thrift plans but only about 13 million actually do.

A 401(k) savings plan is a plan where your employer will match your contribution to savings by a certain percentage. Each time you get paid, a pre-determined percentage is automatically taken out of your check before the taxes are taken out. Your employer then deposits or invests this money in a variety of savings and investment instruments.

To make the 401(k) even more attractive, many participating employers will match your contribution with company money, thus helping you save even more. Under IRS tax laws, total contributions are limited to the lesser of $30,000 or 25% of your annual salary.

Another added benefit is that the interest you earn is tax-free until it is withdrawn. Many people will actually bring home more each month by participating in a 401(k) because the contribution will lower their tax burden.

Check with your company payroll or benefits department.

If your employer does not offer such a plan there are still other options. There are a number of professionally managed savings/investment strategies available through financial planners or stock brokerage houses. You can also develop your own self-managed tax-deferred savings plan at your local bank or credit union. These are called IRAs and Keoghs.

Why Save?

Eat, drink and be merry for tomorrow we die. This old adage appears to be gospel for far too many people. For many, especially those in their twenties and thirties, saving for retirement or children's college expenses is at the bottom of the priority list. What these people don't realize is that the amount they will have for retirement depends greatly on *when* they start their savings ... not on *how much* they put away each month.

For example, let's say at age 30 you decide to put away $1,000 per year or $83 per month into savings. Let's suppose you could get a 6% interest rate on your savings and that inflation averaged 4%. At age 65, your $35,000 in savings contributions would have totalled $118,721. The reason, of course, is compounding interest. If, however, you waited one year, until you were 31, to begin your savings, at age 65 you would have $110,856. That one year cost you $7,865. If you waited until age 55 to start your savings, you would have only $13,181 when you retired ten years later.

Consider now what it will cost you to send your children to college when they graduate from high school. The College Board's 1990-91 Cost Survey states the average cost to attend a public college for four years in 1990 was $33,000. A private college was running $72,000 for four years. These figures, of course, include tuition, books, room and board, and other expenses, but still, that is a lot of money. Now let's look at their projections for ten years from now: $61,000 for a public education, $134,000 for private college. In fifteen years they estimate costs will average $86,000 for public and $187,000 for private school. When are you going to start saving?

Of course, it is important to point out that there are a number of ways to cut costs associated with college or retirement. A student could live at home or apply for a scholarship or financial assistance. A retiree will likely have some income from Social Security assuming the Social Security systems stays in place. (To get a projection of how much you will receive from Social Security, call 800-772-1213). But despite the ways to minimize these rising costs, there is no better way to plan for the future than to save now.

There are savings projection charts in Appendix A that will give you a better idea of how your money can grow based on various interest rates and time periods.

So you've decided to set up a savings plan but you aren't sure where to save. The answer to that will depend on your savings goals. The purpose of both saving and investing is to multiply your money.

The main differences between saving and investing are determined by: the degree of risk, the rate of return, the availability of your money, and the amount of protection you will receive against inflation.

Money in a savings account at a bank or credit union is considered to be safe because you can always get back at least the amount of money you put in. Be sure to bank with an institution that is insured by the Federal Deposit Insurance Corporation (FDIC) or the National Credit Union Association (NCUA). These agencies insure your account up to $100,000.

Most regular savings accounts are convenient, flexible and easy to obtain. Savings accounts, however, typically do not provide tremendous rates of return. If your savings needs to be easily accessible, a regular savings account is probably the way to go.

While the main attraction of savings is security, the major advantage of investing is high money-growth potential. Since investment plans usually carry a higher rate of return than savings plans, they will also carry with them a greater amount of risk.

Government savings bonds, Series EE, (replacing the old Series E) are issued in denominations ranging from $50 to $10,000 and are purchased for one-half the amount of their face value. Government bonds mature at varying rates, typically reaching full maturity in ten years as is the case with Series EE bonds. Series HH bonds (replacing the old Series H) are no longer purchased with cash; they are sold in exchange for Series E or EE bonds in denominations of $500 or more. Series HH bonds are purchased for the full face value and pay interest semiannually. Both series must be held at least 6 months before redeeming.

Treasury *Bills* mature in one year or less. The minimum denomination available is $10,000. Treasury *Bonds* are available in denominations of $1,000 with maturities from one to ten years. Bonds, Bills and Notes issued by the U.S. Government are considered the safest investment because they are backed in full faith by the United States Government. Even with a $4 Trillion federal debt, the United States Government is still considered to be the safest investment in the entire world.

Other savings instruments worth looking into include: Certificates of Deposit (CD's), Mutual Funds, Money Markets, Stocks, Commodities, Options, Real Estate, Precious Metals, Antiques and other collectibles, etc. Remember, the greater the return ... the greater the risk, and vice-versa. Thus if you decide to investigate stocks, options, commodities, real estate or any of the other investing instruments available, it would be wise to first invest some of your time into finding an honest yet aggressive financial planner.

The purpose of this book is not to teach you how to get rich, rich, rich, or to give you investment advice—but rather to give you the basics with which you can then go out, ask the right questions, and make the right decisions. Whatever you decide to do with saving and investing, keep in mind that the earlier you start, the better off you will be. But also keep in mind that it is never too late to start.

When all is said and done, something, even a little savings, will be better than nothing.

For more advice on savings and investing you might want to tune in to the gurus of personal finance, Ken and Daria Dolan. The Dolans are the husband and wife money experts who co-host "Smart Money" on CNBC TV and the daily "Smart Money" radio program broadcasting nationwide.

It Is All Up To You!

As you plan your course of action to total debt elimination, and as you map out your financial future, keep in mind that the steps outlined in these chapters are universal. No matter what it is you want to accomplish, be it cleaning up your credit, establishing a savings plan, or running a marathon, the keys to success are the same. Evaluate where you are today. Decide where you want to be tomorrow. Then devise a plan to take you there. And do not let anyone or anything stand in your way.

"Had I but plenty of money, money enough to spare"—those are the words of Robert Browning. To many money is the vehicle by which they achieve all their worldly desires. For others the motto remains, "Money is the root of all evil." I believe that money is good! Money builds hospitals, schools, and churches. It is true that money cannot buy happiness, but the things that it *will* buy, *might* help to make you happy!

In your quest for riches, try to keep a level head and remember that true wealth is nothing more than a state of mind. Wouldn't it be nice if after we are gone, people would not look back and say, "He was a rich man" or "She was a rich woman." But rather "They were good people, men and women with integrity and an honest desire to help those around them." Remember that true riches are not deposited in a bank account. The riches of the most worth are deposited in the hearts of those around you.

For most of us riches will not come in the form of a Lambourgini. But if that is what you desire, then go for it! Again, there is nothing wrong with money if you are honest while you are getting it, and honest once you've got it. If you're not honest, it probably won't last. Either the government will get you or someone you crossed will. Even if you get away with dishonesty, you won't enjoy your wealth, for you will have no one who appreciates you with which to share it.

To have setbacks is natural. Success cannot be savored if failure is not tasted. Set your goals. Follow the steps outlined in each of these chapters. With patience and perseverance, your debts and financial obligations will become nothing more than vague memories, and your future will be limited only by the size of your dreams.

Amortize To pay off the principal and interest of a loan in equal payments. Although the payments remain the same from month to month, the interest portion of the payment decreases while the principal portion of the payment increases.

Arrears A term used to describe a loan payment or debt that is past due.

Assume To take over the primary responsibility for a mortgage and make the required payments under the original terms of the loan.

Balloon Payment Any payment on a note which is greater than the regular installment payment. A balloon is usually a large principal payment or a payment where the entire balance of the loan is due.

Beneficiary The person, persons, organizations or charities who receives the income from a trustor or the proceeds of a will, trust or estate.

Co-signer A person who signs his or her name to someone else's loan agreement or credit application. The co-signer then agrees to pay the debt in full if the primary signer defaults on the loan.

Collateral Property pledged as security for repayment of a secured debt.

Conventional Mortgage An original, first mortgage made by a mortgage company or lending institution. Usually requires a substantial down payment but the down payment can be reduced by purchasing private mortgage insurance (PMI).

Credit Bureau An agency not affiliated with, but regulated by, the federal government. These agencies gather information on credit users and then sell that information to potential lenders in the form of credit reports.

Credit Rating A point system used by credit bureaus to indicate a person's loan repayment history.

Credit Report A written report prepared by a credit bureau detailing a consumer's credit or loan repayment history. These reports are then sold to potential lenders, insurers and employers.

Deed of Trust A deed by which a trustor conveys legal title to the trustee as security for the payment of a debt.

Discharge	When a consumer's debts are released, or not longer sought for payment, it is called a discharge.
Discount Point	A fee paid by the consumer in return for an interest rate lower than the current market rate. One point typically translates to one percent of the loan amount.
Earnest Money	"Good faith" money put up to show sincerity in a purchase transaction. Earnest money can also be in the form of tangible merchandise such as a car or boat.
Equity	The value of real estate over and above the liens against it.
Escrow Holder	A third party, usually an escrow company, who does the paper work and holds the money for a buyer and seller.
Exempt Property	Property you are allowed to keep if a creditor gets a judgement against you or if you file for bankruptcy.
FHA	The Federal Home Administration. This agency insures portions of loans on homes made by mortgage companies so that buyers can get in for lower down payments.
Garnishment of Wages	Also referred to as "Wage Attachment." This is a method by which you are involuntarily forced to pay off debts through a payroll deduction plan. Under a court order your employer can be forced to deduct payments such as child support, bad debt payments, etc., out of your regular paycheck.
Installment Credit	A credit agreement wherein the consumer agrees to repay a fixed amount of credit in equal payments over a specified period of time. Automobiles, furniture and major appliances are often purchased this way.
Lien	A charge upon the property for the payment of a debt or obligation.
Non-exempt Property	Property you are not allowed to keep if a creditor gets a judgement against you or if you file for bankruptcy.
Prepayment Penalty	A fine imposed in the event of an early payoff of a loan.
Point	See Discount Point
Promissory Note	A written contract containing a promise to pay a definite amount of money at a future time.

136

Revolving Credit   A credit agreement wherein the consumer has the option of paying the balance due, in full, each month or of making partial payments based on the amount of the balance outstanding. There is usually a minimum payment amount required. Once the credit has been repaid, the consumer then has an open line of credit up to a pre-approved limit.

Secured Credit Card   A credit card you obtain by depositing money into a savings account at the bank that issued you the card. If you do not make your payments on the credit card, the bank deducts them from your savings.

Title Insurance   Insurance to protect property owners against loss if the title is imperfect.

Title Company   A company that issues title insurance and acts as an escrow holder when requested.

Trustee   The one who holds the legal title to the property.

Trustor   The owner who is the borrower in a trust deed.

VA Mortgage   A loan on a home originally made to a qualifying veteran of the Armed Services. This type of loan, however, can be assumed by a non-veteran. The Veteran's Administration guarantees part of the loan.

Interest Projections

Ben Franklin said, "The magic of compound interest is that you are first paid interest on your principal and then you are paid interest on your interest." To better illustrate his point, as well as the point made in Chapter Ten, that it matters more *when* you start your savings than *how much* you save each month, look at the following examples. The example on the left shows a 25-year-old investing $2,000 for 9 years and then leaving it to grow at a rate of 10% until the age 65. In the example on the right, investments were not started until age 35. In that example, $2,000 was invested at 10% every year for the next 30 years. The investor on the left contributed $18,000 and ended up with $630,774. The investor on the right contributed $62,000 which grew to $400,275. The moral of the story: Get started as soon as possible!

Age	Amt. Paid In	Equity	Age	Amt. Paid In	Age
25	2,000	2,200	25	0	0
26	2,000	4,620	26	0	0
27	2,000	7,282	27	0	0
28	2,000	10,210	28	0	0
29	2,000	13,431	29	0	0
30	2,000	16,974	30	0	0
31	2,000	20,872	31	0	0
32	2,000	25,159	32	0	0
33	2,000	29,875	33	0	0
34	0	32,862	34	0	0
35	0	36,148	35	2,000	2,200
36	0	39,763	36	2,000	4,620
37	0	43,740	37	2,000	7,282
38	0	48,114	38	2,000	10,210
39	0	52,925	39	2,000	13,431
40	0	58,218	40	2,000	16,974
41	0	64,039	41	2,000	20,872
42	0	70,443	42	2,000	25,159
43	0	77,488	43	2,000	29,875
44	0	85,237	44	2,000	35,062
45	0	93,760	45	2,000	40,769
46	0	103,136	46	2,000	47,045
47	0	113,450	47	2,000	53,950
48	0	124,795	48	2,000	61,545
49	0	137,274	49	2,000	69,899
50	0	151,002	50	2,000	79,089
51	0	166,102	51	2,000	89,198
52	0	182,712	52	2,000	100,318
53	0	200,984	53	2,000	112,550
54	0	221,082	54	2,000	126,005
55	0	243,190	55	2,000	140,805
56	0	267,509	56	2,000	157,086
57	0	294,260	57	2,000	174,995
58	0	323,686	58	2,000	194,694
59	0	356,055	59	2,000	216,364
60	0	391,661	60	2,000	240,200
61	0	430,827	61	2,000	266,420
62	0	473,909	62	2,000	295,262
63	0	521,300	63	2,000	326,988
64	0	573,430	64	2,000	361,887
65	0	630,774	65	2,000	400,275

The chart below shows the results of investing $2,000 at the beginning of each year. The value shown in each column is the value the account will have accumulated at the end of each year. Interest is compounded annually.* The $2,000 figure is used since that is the amount an individual is currently allowed to put in a tax-deferred IRA each year. To use the chart, find the interest rate you expect to receive and the number of years you expect to continue making contributions. The amount in the intersection of those two columns is the amount you will have accumulated.

Value at end of year	5%	6%	8%	10%	12%	14%
1	$ 2,100	$ 2,120	$ 2,160	$ 2,200	$ 2,240	$ 2,280
2	4,305	4,367	4,493	4,620	4,749	4,878
3	6,620	6,749	7,012	7,282	7,559	7,842
4	9,051	9,274	9,733	10,210	10,706	11,220
5	11,604	11,951	12,672	13,431	14,230	15,071
6	14,284	14,788	15,846	16,974	18,178	19,460
7	17,098	17,795	19,273	20,872	22,599	24,464
8	20,053	20,983	22,975	25,159	27,551	30,170
9	23,156	24,362	26,973	29,875	33,097	36,647
10	26,414	27,943	31,291	35,062	39,309	44,087
11	29,834	31,740	35,954	40,769	46,266	52,540
12	33,426	35,764	40,991	47,045	54,058	62,176
13	37,197	40,030	46,430	53,950	62,785	73,162
14	41,157	44,552	52,304	61,545	72,559	85,684
15	45,315	49,345	58,649	69,899	83,507	99,961
16	49,681	54,426	65,500	79,089	95,767	116,234
17	54,265	59,811	72,900	89,198	109,499	134,788
18	59,078	65,520	80,893	100,318	124,879	155,938
19	64,132	71,571	89,524	112,550	142,105	180,048
20	69,439	77,985	98,846	126,005	161,397	207,537
21	75,010	84,785	108,914	140,805	183,005	238,870
22	80,861	91,992	119,787	157,086	207,206	274,594
23	87,004	99,631	131,530	174,995	234,310	315,316
24	96,454	107,729	144,212	194,694	264,668	361,740
25	100,227	116,313	157,909	216,364	298,668	414,665
26	107,338	125,412	172,702	240,200	336,748	474,998
27	114,805	135,056	188,678	266,420	379,398	543,778
28	122,645	145,280	205,932	295,262	427,166	622,186
29	130,878	156,116	224,566	326,988	480,665	711,572
30	139,522	167,603	244,692	361,877	540,585	813,474
35	189,673	236,242	372,204	596,254	966,926	1,581,346
40	253,680	328,095	559,562	973,704	1,718,285	3,059,817

*No adjustment is shown in above totals for income taxes that may be payable upon withdrawal of funds.

This appendix contains copies of the Net Worth Worksheet, Debt Elimination Schedule, Income and Expense charts, Insurance Worksheet, Personal Credit Profile, Daily Expense forms and Monthly Budget chart. Feel free to make extra copies of these charts to insert in your folder or binder.

Net Worth Worksheet
Assets

ASSETS	MARKET VALUE	ASSETS	MARKET VALUE
Cash and Cash Equivalents		**Collectibles**	
Checking account(s)	$_____	Antiques	$_____
Savings account(s)	_____	Art	_____
Certificate(s) of deposit . .	_____	Gold and silver	_____
Money-market account(s) .	_____	Other (stamps, etc.)	_____
Cash mngmnt. account(s)	_____		
Credit union account(s) . .	_____	**Retirement Assets**	
		IRA	_____
Stocks and Bonds		Company pension plan .	_____
Stocks	_____	401(K)	_____
Bonds	_____	Keogh	_____
Futures	_____	Savings plan	_____
Commodities	_____	Profit sharing	_____
Fixed-income securities . .	_____		
Unit trusts	_____	**Insurance**	
Mutual Funds	_____	Cash value-life insurance	_____
Options	_____	Surrender value-annuities	_____
Real-Estate Investment		**Personal Property**	
Value of home	_____	Automobiles	_____
Value of vacation home . .	_____	Boats	_____
Real-estate partnerships . .	_____	Campers/RVs	_____
Rental property	_____	Household furnishing . .	_____
Other	_____	Jewelry	_____
		Other	_____
		Total	$_____

Liabilities

LIABILITIES	PAYOFF BALANCE	LIABILITIES	PAYOFF BALANCE
Home mortgage	$_____	Credit lines	$_____
Vacation home mortgage .	_____	Home equity line	_____
Other real-estate debts . . .	_____	Overdraft line	_____
Automobile loan(s)	_____	Unsecured credit line .	_____
Other installment loan(s) .	_____	Income taxes	_____
Tuition loan(s)	_____	Property taxes	_____
Credit cards:		Margin loans from brokers	_____
Bank	_____	Miscellaneous debt	_____
Retail stores	_____		
Oil companies	_____		
Other	_____	**Total**	$_____

Net Worth

Assets	$_____
Less liabilities	-_____
Net Worth	=$_____

Debt Elimination Schedule
(DES)

	Creditor/Lender	Original Balance	DES Start Date	Current Balance	Monthly Payment	Payoff Balance	Accrued Payment	Projected Payoff
1								
2								
3								
4								
5								
6								
7								
8								
9								
10								
11								
12								
13								
14								
15								
16								
17								
18								
19								
20								
21								
22								
23								
24								
25								
26								
27								
28								
Totals		N/A			N/A	N/A	N/A	

Monthly Earned Income*

Husband . . . . _____

Wife . . . . _____

Children (if helping with expenses) . . . . _____

Self-employed income aside from job . . . . _____

Bonus . . . . _____

Allowance . . . . _____

Interest on savings . . . . _____

Interest from stocks/bonds . . . . _____

Dividends . . . . _____

Rental income . . . . _____

Trust income . . . . _____

Social Security benefits . . . . _____

Veteran's benefits . . . . _____

Pension/retirement income . . . . _____

Unemployment compensation . . . . _____

Disability payments . . . . _____

Assistance payments . . . . _____

Alimony/child support . . . . _____

Gifts/non-obligatory support from family . . . . _____

Other _____ . . . . _____

Other _____ . . . . _____

Other _____ . . . . _____

Other _____ . . . . _____

Other _____ . . . . _____

Total monthly income . . . . $_____

Taxes not withheld that will need to be paid at end of the year . . . _____
(This is the only money to be put in savings)

Total monthly income after taxes . . . . $_____

*List only after-tax, or net income.

Average Monthly Expenses

Rent/mortgage . . . . $ _____

Fuel/gas . . . . _____

Electricity . . . . _____

Water . . . . _____

Garbage . . . . _____

Automobile gasoline/oil/maintenance . . . . _____

Children's expenses—school lunches, fees, etc. . . . . _____

Children's expenses—lessons (piano, dance, etc.) . . . . _____

Children's expenses—other . . . . _____

Higher education/tuition/books . . . . _____

Higher education/room and board . . . . _____

Cable television/pay television channels . . . . _____

Telephone . . . . _____

Pharmacy prescriptions . . . . _____

Medical expenses . . . . _____

Taxes (not already deducted from pay) . . . . _____

Contributions/church . . . . _____

Contributions/savings . . . . _____

Contributions/other . . . . _____

Homeowners/renters insurance . . . . _____

Other property insurance . . . . _____

Disability insurance . . . . _____

Medical/health insurance . . . . _____

Life insurance . . . . _____

Auto insurance . . . . _____

Emergency fund . . . . _____

Allowances . . . . _____

Groceries . . . . _____

Dining out . . . . _____

Laundry/cleaning . . . . _____

Home/office supplies . . . . _____

Animal care . . . . _____

Recreation/entertainment . . . . _____

Travel/vacation . . . . _____

Dues . . . . _____

Subscriptions . . . . _____

Other_____ . . . . _____

Other_____ . . . . _____

Other_____ . . . . _____

Other_____ . . . . _____

Other_____ . . . . _____

Total monthly expenses . . . . $ _____

Life Insurance Worksheet

I. Cash Needs
    A. Funeral and burial expenses $ _____
    B. Probate and estate taxes   _____
       (Estimate 5% of gross estate.)
    C. Outstanding debts, including home mortgage.   _____
       (Use the total from the Current Balance column
       of your Debt Elimination Schedule on page 29.)
    D. Emergency fund   _____
       (Equal to three months of your total take home pay.)
    E. *College fund (Current cost of college for four   _____
       years multiplied by the number of children.)

       Total (lines A through E)   = _____

II. Annual Income Needs
    A. Annual income needed to maintain your family's   _____
       current standard of living.
       (Figure 75-80% of your current gross income.)
    B. Less annual Social Security benefits to be paid   - _____
       to your surviving dependents. (Call the Social
       Security Department at 800-772-1213 for an
       estimate of your annual S.S. benefit.)
    C. Less spouse's annual income   - _____
    D. Less any other annual income (Estimated   - _____
       investment/IRA distributions.)

       Total (Item IIA minus items IIB, IIC, & IID)   = _____

III. Retirement plan for spouse/family
    A. Amount from total at end of Section II.   _____
    B. Multiply amount from the line above by the   = _____
       number of years income will be needed.
       (Example assumes 20 years.)

IV. Available assets
    A. Assets currently available (Cash, stocks, etc.)   _____

V. Insurance Needed
    A. Cash needs from total in Section I.   _____
    B. Plus annual income/retirement needs from
       Section IIIB.   + _____
    C. Minus available assets from Section IV.   - _____

       Total insurance needed.   = _____
       (Item A plus item B, minus item C.)

NOTE:
  This worksheet is for illustrative purposes only. To determine your exact insurance needs you should consult with an estate planning attorney or financial planner.

*   In the event of your death, insurance proceeds in this amount would be deposited as a lump sum into a savings/investment account until needed. It is assumed that interest earned during the interim should exceed the rate of inflation, thereby maintaining the same purchasing power.

PERSONAL CREDIT PROFILE

	Creditor/Lender	Credit Limit	Interest Rate	Annual Fee	Grace Period	Secured Yes/No	Equity Built Up	Rating +/-/?
1								
2								
3								
4								
5								
6								
7								
8								
9								
10								
11								
12								
13								
14								
15								
16								
17								
18								
19								
20								
21								
22								
23								
24								
25								
26								
27								
28								
Totals			**N/A**		**N/A**	**N/A**		**N/A**

The Spending Plan
Daily Expense Forms

Daily Expenses	Date:
Item	Cost
	Total

Daily Expenses	Date:
Item	Cost
	Total

Daily Expenses	Date:
Item	Cost
	Total

Daily Expenses	Date:
Item	Cost
	Total

MONTHLY BUDGET

	Month _____			Month _____		
	Amount Estimated	Amount Spent	Difference	Amount Estimated	Amount Spent	Difference
Rent/Mortgage						
Phone						
Utilities						
Groceries						
Dining Out						
Clothing						
Auto Repairs						
Gas and oil						
Parking/tolls						
Bus and taxi						
Credit Card 1						
Credit Card 2						
Credit Card 3						
Auto Loan						
Personal Loan 1						
Personal Loan 2						
Student Loan						
Other Loan 1						
Other Loan 2						
Life Insurance						
Health Insurance						
Property Ins.						
Auto Insurance						
Disability Ins.						
Tuition/Fees						
Books						
Medical/Dental						
Child Care						
Recreation						
Emergency Fund						
Savings						
IRAs						
Investments						
Gifts						
Miscellaneous						
Total Income:						
Total Expenses:						
Difference:						

The following letters are for illustrative purposes only and should not be copied word for word. Credit bureaus, banks, creditors and just about everyone else (myself included) do not like to get form letters, and rarely are they treated with the attention you will need while trying to clean-up your personal credit profile. Instead, use the examples provided as guidelines to help you as you prepare your own correspondence during the clean-up process.

You should also note that these and the other forms contained in this manual do not constitute legal or binding contracts or correspondence. Thus you should not try to convey to creditors, credit bureaus or any other individuals or organizations that they are such. You may find it necessary to consult an attorney if your situation is complex or out of the ordinary.

CONSUMER LETTER REQUESTING A COPY
OF CREDIT REPORT

Today's Date

Credit Bureau Name
Street Address
City, State ZIP
Attn: Credit Reports

Dear Sir or Madam:

I am in the process of making some adjustments in my financial portfolio and need a copy of my credit report to help with some of the decisions I am facing. I would appreciate it if you would send a copy of my report that is on file with your agency. Enclosed is a check for $____ to cover the cost. The following identifying information should help you fulfill my request.

1. Full name
2. Name of spouse
3. Current complete address
4. Previous complete address
5. Social Security number
6. Social Security number of spouse
7. Date of birth
8. Date of birth for spouse

Thank you for your cooperation and speedy reply.

Sincerely,

Your Name

CONSUMER LETTER REQUESTING A COPY
OF CREDIT REPORT AFTER BEING
DENIED CREDIT

Today's Date

Credit Bureau Name
Street Address
City, State ZIP
Attn: Credit Reports

Dear Sir or Madam:

I was recently denied credit by __(company or creditor)__ based on a credit report provided by your agency. I would like to know what is in my credit file and would appreciate your providing me with this information.

I understand that according to the *Fair Credit Reporting Act*, because I have been denied credit within that last 60 days, there will be no charge for this information.

I have included a copy of my rejection notice. The following information is for identification purposes.

1. Full name
2. Name of spouse
3. Current complete address
4. Previous complete address
5. Social Security number
6. Social Security number of spouse
7. Date of birth
8. Date of birth for spouse

Thank you for your cooperation and prompt attention to this matter.

Sincerely,

Your Name

CONSUMER LETTER REQUESTING INVESTIGATION
OF AN ALLEGED ERROR

Today's Date

Credit Bureau Name
Street Address
City, State ZIP
Attn: Credit Reports

Dear Sir or Madam:

The following information on my credit report is incorrect since I have not had any dealing with __(company name)__ .

SAM'S STEREO SYSTEMS   Account #123456789

The *Fair Credit Reporting Act* requires that you examine this dispute and update my report with the corrected information. I understand that federal law also requires you to provide me with the names and addresses of each company and individual you checked with during your investigation.

Thank you for your cooperation. I look forward to receiving the results of your inquiry in a timely manner.

Sincerely,

Your name
Social Security number
Date of birth

Sample Letter #4

CONSUMER LETTER REQUESTING INVESTIGATION
OF AN ALLEGED ERROR

Today's Date

Credit Bureau Name
Street Address
City, State ZIP
Attn: Credit Reports

Dear Sir or Madam:

My credit report lists inaccurate information for the following account. (Be specific about inaccuracies.)

SEAGULL STATE BANK   **Mortage# 98765**

Please investigate this account and remove the incorrect data from my file. I understand that according to the *Fair Credit Reporting Act*, your bureau must investigate this account within a "reasonable time" and inform me of the results.

I understand that a list of the names and addresses of those you contacted during your investigation should be sent to me along with an updated copy of my credit report. I also understand that any company, individual or organization that has requested a copy of my credit report within the last six months should also be sent a copy of the updated information.

Thank you for your cooperation and speedy reply.

Sincerely,

Your name
Social Security number
Date of birth

CONSUMER LETTER TO REMIND
CREDIT BUREAU OF YOUR REQUEST

Today's Date

Credit Bureau Name
Street Address
City, State ZIP
Attn: Credit Reports

Dear Sir or Madam:

I recently sent a letter to your bureau asking that an incorrect item listed on my credit report be investigated. The *Fair Credit Reporting Act* requires that you respond to my dispute within a reasonable amount of time. I am wondering why I have not yet received a response from you.

Please examine my request and remove the inaccurate information from my record. Also, a list of names and addresses for companies and individuals you used in this investigation should be supplied to me. The entry/account in question is:

CARLA'S USED CARS   **ACCT. #29331**

This erroneous information is causing me concern as it is damaging my credit and my reputation. I would appreciate your immediate attention to this matter.

Sincerely,

Your name
Social Security number
Date of birth

P.S. A copy of this letter has been sent to the Federal Trade Commission, Division of Consumer Credit, Washington, D.C. 20580

CONSUMER LETTER REQUESTING THAT
A COLLECTION AGENCY OR COLLECTOR
END FURTHER COMMUNICATION

Today's date

Collection Agency Name
Street Address
City, State ZIP

Dear Sir or Madam:

As per our last telephone conversation, I maintain that I do not owe the alleged debt to
  (creditor) . Thus I wish to end all communication with you and your
representatives.   I understand under the *Fair Debt Collection Practices Act* that it is
my right to demand that you not contact me or members of my family further
regarding this matter.

Respectfully,

Your name

Look for the "Target" Personal Finance Computer Software Program at your local computer software store, office supply or bookstore. Or you can use this order form to request additional copies of <u>Till Debt Due Us Part</u>, the "Target" software program, or related <u>Till Debt Due Us Part</u> products. When ordering Debt Elimination Schedules and Amortization Schedules be sure to include the forms on the following pages. DES and Amortization loan information forms must be completed in their entirety.

Order Form

Name

Address (UPS to street address, Priority Mail to P.O. boxes)

Quantity	Item	Unit Price	Total

Price List:

Till Debt Due Us Part $ 16.95
Target computer software   34.95
Debt Elimination Schedule 5.00
Amortization Schedule   2.00
Shipping & handling   3.50

Subtotal	
Sales Tax (Utah residents add 6¼%)	
Shipping & handling	
TOTAL	

PRICES SUBJECT TO CHANGE

Send check or money order to:
D.C. Publishers & Management, L.C.
P.O. Box 21958
Salt Lake City, Utah 84121-0958
Phone or FAX (801) 224-0670

To order using ☐VISA or ☐MasterCard:

Account #: _____

Expiration Date: _____

Signature: _____

Phone: _____

Debt Elimination Schedule
Information Form
(This form must accompany your order.)

Creditor/Lender	Plan Start Date	Current Balance	Monthly Payment	Interest Rate

Amortization Schedule
Information Form
(This form must accompany your order.)

Creditor	Original Balance	Date of 1st payment	Number of years financed	Interest Rate	Current Balance	Number of payments per year	Payment Amount

Note: Amortization Schedules are $2.00 each. Each line of information is <u>one</u> schedule.

Index

F

Fair Credit Reporting Act 78-79, 81-83, 163-165
Fair Debt Collection Practices Act 85-87, 166
Federal Debt 10
Federal Deposit Insurance Corporation (FDIC) 131
Federal Trade Commission 72, 88, 165
Finance Charges, 97
Financial Planners 58-59, 132

G

Goals 14-17, 82, 91, 101, 109, 111, 133
Government Savings Bonds 131
Grace Period 72, 105-108

H

Health Insurance 58
Home Mortgages 27, 43-50, 53, 58, 124
Hybrid Insurance 61

I

Installment Credit 74-75, 136
Insurance 27, 28, 30, 65, 125, 137
    Disability Insurance 63-64
    Health Insurance 58, 63
    Non-Renewable Term 60
    Renewable Term 60
    Term Insurance 60-63
    Universal Life 61
    Variable Life 61
    Whole Life 60-61
Interest 10, 21, 24, 31-32, 37, 43-50, 84, 95-97, 105-108, 121, 127, 129, 131-132, 139
Interest Projections 139-140
Interest Rates 31, 32, 48-49, 97, 129, 136
Internal Revenue Service (IRS) 21
IRAs 21, 23, 59, 63

L

Liabilities 23-24
Life Insurance 23, 28, 30, 57-63
Living Expenses 27, 28, 31, 59, 99
Loan Applications 125

M

Monthly Budgets 114-115
Monthly Earned Income 29
Monthly Payment 24-26, 31-38, 45, 46, 48, 127
Mortgages 27, 30, 43-50, 53, 69, 135-137

N

National Credit Union Association (NCUA) 131
National Debt 10
National Foundation for Consumer Credit 88
Negative Credit Instruments 111
Net Worth 22-23
Net Worth Worksheet 23
Non-debt 27
Non-exempt Property 40-41, 136
Non-Renewable Term 60

O

Open 30-day Agreement 74
Open End Credit 91-92
Order Form 167
Original Balance 24-26, 33-37

P

Payment History 74
Payoff Balance 23-25, 33-37
Personal Credit Profile 105, 106, 108, 110, 117, 141
Premiums 60-63
Probate 59, 65
Projected Payoff 24, 25, 33-37

R

Refinancing 48-50, 108
Renewable Term 60
Revolving Credit 74, 76, 91, 94, 97, 137
Rotating Bank Method 126
Rules 20, 64, 71

S

Sample Credit Report 75-76
Sample Letters 72